*

VEGAN
TREATS

For Azaria Primrose, my sweetest bake yet

VEGAN TREATS

Easy vegan bites & bakes

GLUTEN FREE, DAIRY FREE & REFINED-SUGAR FREE

EMMA HOLLINGSWORTH

PHOTOGRAPHS BY JEN RICH

Kyle Books

Contents

HOW IT ALL BEGAN

I've got a serious sweet tooth, a mouth full of them in fact. My birthdays as a child were filled with cakes of dreams—the hedgehog cake with chocolate buttons for spikes, the treasure chest cake filled with chocolate coins and the classic Victoria sponge. But that doesn't mean I've always been into baking—far from it. When I left university in 2008, unable to rustle up so much as a basic stir-fry, the thought of baking a cake was way beyond my comfort zone. My standard day was comprised of a small inadequate breakfast, a bag of chocolates from the university shop for an "al desko" lunch in the library, followed by a liquid dinner.

After university, I moved back to London and started a graduate scheme at a top accountancy firm, where Emma Friedman, a Jewish girl from North West London, met Richard Hollingsworth, a fun-loving, beer-drinking, rugby-playing "wide boy" from Essex. Two years on when Mr. H had moved into my little apartment in Chalk Farm, I was living a healthier(ish) life. I'd go to the gym before work and have yogurt and granola for breakfast, then a salad for lunch, and I actually knew where the kitchen was in my apartment. But for all my "healthy" lifestyle changes, I still wasn't feeling amazing. My energy levels were low; my hair, skin, and nails weren't as glowing as I wanted them to be; my moods were all over the place; and by 8 every evening I look liked I was very much "with child."

I suspected my diet might still be to blame, so I went to see a specialist for some tests, as well as my GP. I had always suspected that I had IBS, and I was right. I also found out that I was lactose intolerant. What's more, my test results showed that I had polycystic ovary syndrome, which explained years of irregular cycles, so it was suggested that I steer clear of refined sugar, as this can lead to hormonal imbalances, which can worsen the symptoms. I had some serious apologizing to do to my body, so decided to give it a go, and to give up caffeine while I was at it.

To my surprise, I began to enjoy my foray into the world of natural foods and healthy cuisine. Every day I would plan my dinner using recipes online. Savory recipes weren't so much of a challenge. I had always liked veggies, so I would heap our plates full of a rainbow of goodness, with lots of grains and healthy fats. I discovered a whole world of spices, learned how to pronounce "quinoa," and discovered that the weird storage cupboard thing under my stovetop was actually an oven.

But sweet stuff just wasn't so easy. Long before Mr. H and I shared a surname, we shared a very serious, deep, and all-encompassing love. Of chocolate. So neither of us was happy about the lack of chocolate bars, cookies, and the like in our apartment. I decided to try my hand at devising and making my own desserts, and bought myself a cheap food processor. The list of fails is too long to detail, but there was the carrot cake that tasted just of carrot, the gloopy chia puddings, the rock-hard cookies . . . when I finally mastered banana bread, I realized that with all the expensive nuts and other ingredients, I had spent almost $25.

I felt sure there had to be a simpler, more cost-effective way, so I made it my mission to find one. My family was dubious when I first offered them things to test, but after a little persistence they started to enjoy trialing my creations, and the feedback was fast improving. My friends at work were enjoying it, too. And Mr. H? He was loving it! I started writing up my simple, budget-friendly recipes, and when my wonderful friend Effie suggested we start a blog one day, I jumped at the chance. She shared her insights on mindfulness and wellness, while I provided the food content.

Having left my horribly stressful job in 2015 to concentrate on trying to start a family, I eventually became pregnant and decided to make myself busy with my recipes. I started selling some desserts for next to nothing to some local cafés, and felt very proud that I was earning all of $25 a week because I was doing something I loved. After a magical pregnancy, I gave birth to Azaria Primrose Hollingsworth, aka Baby H, under a strawberry moon, in a birth pool, on one Tylenol. Soon after, one of the cafés I supplied asked me for their weekly order. I hate letting people down, so I went into the kitchen and back to work.

During this time, I was also studying at the Institute of Integrative Nutrition in order to become a certified health coach. I learned not only about foods themselves and different diets, but most important about how people's relationships with food are determined by so many other things in their lives. The principles I learned helped me repair my own relationship with food, and I also realized that I was applying them when creating my recipes.

Once Baby H was a few months old, I knew that it was time to develop Mrs. Hollingsworth's into a full-fledged business, so I applied to a nearby little farmers' market. Every Saturday morning I was there with all my delicious wares, and my dad would potter up the hill from his house to help me. I can't tell you how cold it was after five hours standing still, but it was also so much fun, and I met some interesting and amazing people; Emma Thompson even popped by one week to buy lots of treats for a family gathering! The best thing about it was my littlest customers. There seem to be many children with food intolerances these days and quite often they can't have the yummy things their friends enjoy, so to see their faces light up when I told them that everything on my stall was free from eggs, dairy, gluten, and sugar was very heartwarming.

Once I had honed my product range, I approached Ethos Foods near Oxford Circus to see if they might like to sell any of my treats. They were keen to set up a meeting, and when they tried the samples I brought them, it was an immediate yes! I was soon supplying them, and other local cafés, with over 500 desserts a week from my little kitchen. The demand for my celebration cakes was also increasing, and I decided to start running monthly baking classes around my kitchen table, where I teach people my recipes and show them just how easy it is to make healthier free-from treats.

With lots of people inquiring online about when I would be sharing my recipes in a book, I decided it was time to embark on this project. I hope that as you read it you will realize that healthier eating doesn't need to mean bland, tasteless desserts, nor does it require expensive ingredients that can't be found in your local supermarket, nor indeed does it need to be complicated in the slightest.

One more thing. Anyone who reads my blog will know how much I love telling the stories behind my recipes, what or who inspired them and how they came about. You might also know that I love a pun. So apologies in advance if you don't, because this book is lit(t)erally littered with them. I just can't help myself!

GETTING STARTED IN THE KITCHEN

First things first—do you know where your kitchen is? OK, good. Now, before we get ourselves knee-deep in cake mixture, I thought it might be useful to tell you a little bit about what I reckon are the best gadgets and gizmos when it comes to healthy baking, as well as the ingredients that I just can't live without.

FOOD PROCESSORS

The vast majority of my recipes do tend to require some pulsing or processing. This is due to the nature of the lovely natural whole foods in said recipes because, although ingredients like nuts and dates are totally delicious, they do tend to be pretty chunky, and no amount of stirring or whisking is going to change that.

My first food processor was a Kenwood one, which was pretty reasonably priced and good quality too. But as I began to bake more and more, I realized I needed something a little bigger and more powerful. Enter Maggie, my Magimix, who has been happily sat on my kitchen worktop for about three years now, whizzing away a good couple of times a day and showing no signs of stopping any time soon. The other machine that I use every day is my Vitamix, a high-speed blender that can, for example, make hot soup from scratch and instant ice cream. It's amazing for whizzing up

items of a more liquid consistency— sauces, caramel, "cheesecake" mixtures, frostings—although all of these can also be made in a good food processor. However, it can get a bit upset if it needs to blend something that is tougher in texture like dates, so if you are going to get just one machine, a food processor covers all bases.

OTHER USEFUL KIT

Besides the basics of mixing bowls and parchment paper, cake pans and loaf pan are pretty handy, as are silicone molds and paper liners. I seriously rate silicone chocolate mold trays, as all you need to do is pour your chocolate mixture into them and pop them in the fridge to set, after which they come out looking all heart-/star-/seashell-shaped and super fancy. I buy most of these on Amazon, as they are usually available for next-day delivery and it saves me from hunting them down in the stores.

MEASURING MADE EASY

My recipes are all about keeping things simple, so I don't tend to use kitchen scales, which in my opinion are a bit of a faff. Instead I use measuring cups, tablespoons, and teaspoons. I'm sure you have the latter two in your kitchen, but if you don't have measuring cups, they are easily available and a great time saver. It's good to know that 1 cup = 16 tablespoons, so if, for example, you need ¼ cup of something or other but your measuring cups have gone AWOL, you can just measure out 4 table-spoons. However, just in case you do want conversions, the chart opposite features my most-used ingredients.

CUP CONVERSIONS

INGREDIENT	¼ CUP	⅓ CUP	½ CUP	1 CUP
almonds, whole	1¼oz	1¾oz	2½oz	5oz
almonds, ground	¾oz	1¼oz	1¾oz	3½oz
buckwheat flour	1oz	1½oz	2oz	4¼oz
cacao nibs	1oz	1½oz	2oz	4¼oz
cacao powder	¾oz	1¼oz	1¾oz	3½oz
cacao butter	2oz	2¾oz	4oz	8oz
cashews, whole	1¼oz	1½oz	2¼oz	4½oz
coconut milk	2oz	1½oz	4¼oz	8½oz
coconut, desiccated	¾oz	1¼oz	1¾oz	3½oz
coconut oil	1¾oz	2½oz	3½oz	7oz
dates, Medjool and dried	¼oz	1¾oz	2½oz	5¼oz
hazelnuts, whole	1oz	1½oz	2oz	4¼oz
maple syrup	2¾oz	3¾oz	5½oz	11¼oz
nut butters	2oz	2¾oz	4¼oz	8½oz
oats, rolled	¾oz	1¼oz	1¾oz	3½oz
peanuts, whole	1¼oz	1¾oz	2½oz	5oz
pecans, halves	¾oz	1¼oz	1¾oz	3½oz
pistachio nuts, whole	1¼oz	1½oz	2¾oz	4½oz
walnuts, halves	¾oz	1¼oz	1¾oz	3½oz

PANTRY ESSENTIALS

Although in this book you will find an array of different ingredients, I wanted to explore in a little more depth my absolute essentials, many of which form the foundation of my recipes.

NUTS & NUT BUTTERS

If you are what you eat, then I'm totally nuts. If you are not on it already, I urge you to hop aboard the nut train, unless you are allergic to nuts, in which case don't get on at all costs. Speaking of allergies, many of my recipes do use nuts, but look out for the 'nut free' label for ones that don't. Always check your ingredients if you're allergic.

ALMONDS Almonds make good milk. Fact. It's becoming more and more commonplace these days to find almond milk in cafés and supermarkets, but often it contains lots of unnecessary ingredients. Some brands make great almond milk with natural ingredients only, but they can be expensive, especially compared to making a batch at home with a handful of almonds, a nut milk bag, and some water (see page 18).

Ground almonds are great in baking, and make an ideal replacement for ordinary flour. I buy preground almonds in bulk online, but you can also pulse whole nuts in a food processor to make your own.

CASHEWS These are the creamiest nuts in the business, and once soaked in water for a few hours, they can be drained and blended to make the most amazing frostings and "cheesecakes." I love to use cashew butter in my recipes, too, as it adds a milkier flavor to things like raw chocolate and is also great for making white chocolate (see page 31).

PEANUTS I know peanuts are technically a legume, but I've popped them into this category anyway. I've been an "eat peanut butter with a spoon out of the jar" kinda gal since I can remember, and when I realized it could be used in dessert making, my world was complete. It also tends to be the cheapest of the nut butters, so if you are limiting your spend on ingredients, you can substitute it for the different nut butters in most of my recipes.

HAZELNUTS An essential nut if you grew up slathering a popular hazelnut-chocolate spread on your toast in the mornings, as I did, and you want to re-create a healthier version. Hazelnut butter, though, is rather expensive (albeit totally divine), so I don't tend to cook with it much for that reason.

PECANS, WALNUTS & PISTACHIOS I don't use these nuts quite as often as the others, but they do still feature in my cooking because sometimes it's just nice to mix things up a bit. And who doesn't like a slice of pecan pie in the autumn or a gooey walnut brownie on days of the week that end with the letter "y"? Exactly.

NATURALLY SWEET

There are some amazing, affordable, and delicious alternatives to refined white sugar, as well as some not-so-budget-friendly ones. I tend to stay away from things like coconut nectar, date syrup, and agave because either I can't find them in my local supermarket, or they are expensive or just don't taste that good. Agave has quite a high glycaemic index, meaning it can cause more of a spike and then a crash in blood sugar levels (as sugar does).

DATES The beautiful sweet, caramel flavor of dates makes them an amazing baking staple. Their stickiness lends itself to fudgy brownies, chewy energy balls and tantalizing raw tarts, and can also be blended to make gorgeous caramels and sauces. Medjools are my date of choice, as they are a lot softer and juicer than other dried dates and are easier to work with. But with all that deliciousness comes a heftier price tag, so if you are sticking with the less expensive kind, it's best to soak them in some warm water for about 10 minutes before you use them, otherwise your food processor may complain.

PURE MAPLE SYRUP
Look for the words "pure" and "grade A" on the label of maple syrup, avoiding the "normal" kind, which is sweetened with things like corn syrup, so isn't pure. It's a little more expensive, but so much better health- and taste-wise.

OTHER NATURAL SWEETENERS
Although I use dates or pure maple syrup in the majority of my recipes, I often use other sweet ingredients to complement these in my baking, such as cinnamon, a lovely, delicious warming spice in banana breads or carrot cakes. Cinnamon also helps to stabilize and regulate blood sugar, so it's a great ingredient to pack into your granola bars or breakfast muffins to stave off any sugar cravings later in the day. Vanilla is also an awesome ingredient for adding a depth of flavor and a little extra sweetness, but be careful to buy "pure vanilla extract" rather than "vanilla essence," as the latter can contain synthetic flavorings. It's relatively expensive, but a little goes a long way.

Fruits such as mashed bananas and pureed apples make great natural sugar substitutes, as well as providing valuable binding qualities (see page 14).

COCONUT LOVE

Oil, cream, milk, desiccated . . . coconut in all its forms is the wonder ingredient of free-from baking. I use coconut oil to grease my baking pans instead of butter, melted in frostings and "cheesecakes" to make them set and, most important, in dark chocolate making (see page 31). Coconut cream makes the best dairy cream substitute, and is great in frostings, truffles and "cheesecakes." The only coconut products I'm not totally down with are coconut sugar (expensive and hard to find, so you will only see it in two recipes in this book) and coconut flour (also expensive and elusive, and very crumbly and dry in most recipes).

A BOUQUET OF FLOURS

I know there is such a thing as "gluten-free flour," but I don't trust it as far as I can throw it, which isn't very far, as bags of flour are pretty heavy. I love buckwheat flour for its nutty and rich flavor, but I'm also a massive fan of almond flour (ground almonds) and oat flour (ground oats). I sometimes use peanut flour too, if I'm making something and I want it to be really peanutty.

To make your own flours, simply pop your nuts or oats into a food processor or high-speed blender and quickly process until a fine flour forms (just don't overprocess the nuts into nut butter!). You can then store this flour in airtight containers and bake with it to your heart's content!

GRAINS

Oats are my favorite grain in the business. I have porridge for breakfast most mornings. I love making creamy oat milk and use oats as a key component in my flapjacks and granola. They are super cheap to buy, too, although the "gluten-free" ones can be a little more expensive. Speaking of which, there is a common misconception that oats = gluten. Oats do not actually contain gluten, but many oats can't be certified gluten-free because they are made in facilities that also handle products containing gluten, so there could be cross-contamination. If you are following a gluten-free diet but do not have celiac disease or another gluten-intolerance, then ordinary oats are fine to use.

I don't use other grains quite as much in my baking, but puffed brown rice and toasted buckwheat groats are great for creating crispy and crunchy textures.

HOW NOW BROWN CACAO

I am totally, ridiculously, completely, insanely obsessed with chocolate. And it is pretty mind-blowing when you think that both cacao powder and cacao butter come from the same cacao pod. These are the two key ingredients in making raw chocolate, so the pods are basically a deconstructed chocolate bar in its raw form!

I'll be showing you how to make white, "milk," and dark raw chocolate on page 31. You'll see that sometimes I use cacao butter as the oil ingredient in chocolate making and other times I use coconut oil. I prefer the taste of coconut oil, and it's cheaper and more readily available than cacao butter. However, it has a lower melting point, which means that anything you make with it will melt a little more easily, so I would definitely recommend using cacao butter if your creations are going to be outside the fridge for a while during the summer months.

HIMALAYAN PINK SALT

You might think I'm totally losing the plot talking about salt in a sweet cookbook, but it's actually often a key ingredient, as it helps to enhance sweet, spicy, fruity or nutty flavors. A little pinch of salt really goes a long way in baking, and I like to use Himalayan pink salt, as it is purer than normal table salt; plus, it contains over 83 different minerals. And it's pink, so what's not to like?

FLAXSEEDS AND CHIA SEEDS

These little seeds are my secret weapon when it comes to replacing eggs. You will see that some of my recipes call for flaxseed or chia "eggs." For each flaxseed or chia "egg," simply mix 1 tablespoon ground flaxseeds or 1 tablespoon chia seeds with 3 tablespoons water and let sit for 10 minutes, or until you have a gloopy mixture. Chia seeds also make a great addition to homemade jelly and give it a wonderful texture, as you will discover in my Berry Chia Jelly recipe (page 26).

SUPERFOOD POWDERS

"Superfoods" can be extremely expensive, as they are usually very concentrated powders imported from the depths of the Amazon (the rain forest, not the website) or somewhere similarly exotic. While there is evidence that these are good for you, you won't find them as key ingredients in my recipes because I like to keep things as simple and budget-friendly as possible, and also because you can get amazing nutrients from delicious healthy foods that haven't been branded as "super."

That said, I do love using superfood powders as plant-based colorings for frostings and "cheesecakes." See the chart below for my favorites, which are great for introducing some jazzy colors into your desserts or when you are making a celebration cake (see pages 150–156). Some, like turmeric, you can find in your local supermarket for under $1.50, while others (butterfly pea powder, I'm looking at you) are only available online. I use them more for color than for flavor, so don't worry if you can't find a particular item, as your desserts will taste just as scrumptious.

NATURAL FOOD COLORING SUBSTITUTES

NATURAL SUBSTITUTE	FOR
beet or pink pitaya powder	red/pink food coloring
matcha green tea, wheatgrass, or spirulina powder	green food coloring
turmeric or carrot powder	yellow food coloring
butterfly pea powder	blue food coloring
activated charcoal powder	black food coloring

BAKING WITH FRUITS, VEGGIES & LEGUMES

Adding fruits and vegetables to vegan cakes works so well because not only can they help with binding the mixture, as eggs traditionally do, but they also keep the texture really light and moist.

In terms of shopping organically, I am guided by the EWG's "Clean Fifteen" and "Dirty Dozen" lists, updated annually, that detail which items are, respectively, the least and most affected by herbicides and pesticides. Fruits such as bananas and avocados, for example, have thick skins, so any chemicals used by farmers are less likely to have passed into their produce, whereas thinner-skinned fruits like apples, berries, and peaches, can often be contaminated with chemicals. Therefore, I try to buy the latter grown organically whenever I can.

BANANAS Banana is a fabulous egg replacement, not just in banana breads but in many other desserts, helping to bind mixtures as well as preventing baked goods from becoming dry. Bananas can also be used in frostings and blended from frozen into amazing ice cream. Overripe bananas have the best texture and are even better for you than less ripe ones, as they are easier to digest and contain higher levels of antioxidants.

APPLES & PEARS These are also a great egg replacer in cakes, especially useful if you are allergic to bananas. Pureed apple and pear are relatively mild tasting in baking, so they won't overpower other flavors.

BERRIES I love using berries in baking to add a little tartness, and they complement sweet flavors really well. I try to buy my berries in season where possible and freeze them, as you can bake with them from frozen, and they also taste better.

AVOCADO The creamy texture of avocado makes it an ideal dairy substitute in frostings and mousses. Just make sure your avocados are nice and ripe.

ZUCCHINI, CARROTS, BEETS & SWEET POTATOES You might be a little skeptical, but I promise you that when it comes to cakes, these guys are amazing. There is so much goodness to be had from them in terms of antioxidants and vitamins, but they also add a rainbow of amazing colors and flavors to desserts.

LEGUMES Not only are these super cheap, all you need do is open the can, drain the contents, and chuck them in. I love black beans in brownies (see page 57), and chickpeas make delicious blondies (see page 58) and cookies, too. Prepare to bean amazed.

SMART SHOPPING

Buying in bulk is a great way to save money on ingredients; Medjool dates, cacao powder, and pure maple syrup are cheaper in large quantities. In the US, try Costco. They are the cheapest around and of amazing quality. I also really rate Amazon, which sells things like nut butters in big tubs. You can also subscribe for certain items, for example, a tub of cashew butter once a month, yielding a further discount. Other websites such as Thrive Market and Vitacost are also great.

Although in theory bulk buying makes sense, it can be tricky on storage space. One friend of mine gets together with her neighbors and splits purchases, so they all benefit from the cheaper prices but save on space. Another, albeit unlikely, tip I have for you is comparison websites. MyGroceryDeals compares prices of products so that you can see what is on sale where and stock up.

I buy mixing bowls, baking sheets, measuring cups, and paper liners for my baking courses from my local dollar store—give yours a visit if you are just getting started.

FREE-FROM BAKING SUBSTITUTES

The table below explains which traditional ingredients can be replaced with other plant-based foods. It really is possible to create free-from versions of everything when it comes to desserts!

FREE-FROM SUBSTITUTE	FOR
buckwheat flour ground almonds ground oats desiccated coconut	wheat flour
coconut milk avocado	dairy cream
flaxseed and chia seed "eggs" bananas	eggs
nut and seed butters coconut oil	dairy butter
nut, oat, and coconut milks	dairy milk
soaked cashews	cream cheese in "cheesecakes" and frostings

WHAT YOU WILL FIND IN THIS BOOK

While 100 percent of the recipes in this book can be classified as "vegan," they are not just for vegans—they're for everyone. They are for people who want to eat indulgent and delicious desserts using only natural ingredients and whole foods, with no additives, preservatives, or substances your body might not thank you for adding. They are for families and friends, young and old, who want to enjoy the sweeter things in life. They are for busy worker bees and supermamas who don't have loads of time on their hands but want to make something quick, simple, and tasty to satisfy their sweet tooth.

I also want to touch briefly on the concept of "bio-individuality," whereby food that nourishes one person may be another person's poison. After years of not listening to my body, when I finally tuned into my natural rhythm, I realized that gluten, dairy, and refined sugars don't really work for me. Equally, I know people who absolutely swear by dairy and who can eat gluten without feeling the slightest bit bloated afterward. If you suspect you might be intolerant to certain foods, it's important to consult your GP as well as a nutritionist to make sure that you continue getting all the nutrients your body needs.

I am passionate about sharing with as many people as possible the message that healthier, free-from baking doesn't need to cost the earth, and shouldn't involve making pilgrimages to far-flung health food stores for obscure ingredients that will be used once and then left to collect dust in your kitchen cupboards. Very few of my recipes require more than ten different ingredients because, if you are anything like me, seeing that you need to source a list of things as long as your arm can be enough to put you right off.

That said, being the creator of bespoke celebration cakes, I also want to use this opportunity to show you how easy and simple it is (not to mention cheaper) to create showstopping cakes for yourself (see pages 150–156). These cakes can be adapted to be as simple or as decorative as you like, and can also be made in stages if you only have an hour to grab here or there. I can't wait to see what amazing creations you come up with!

This chapter includes some of my most often made and useful concoctions. Each one is incredibly simple but wonderfully tasty, and they are referred to a lot throughout the remainder of the book.

Not a week goes by without me making the majority of these recipes; I use homemade milks for everything from porridge to puddings, go through nut butters and homemade jelly like there is no tomorrow, pour chocolate sauce and salted caramel over anything and everything, and top my cakes and cupcakes with an array of delicious frostings.

This chapter is what you could call my little box of tricks—as well as being amazing on their own, these recipes are also the finishing touches on so many other desserts and sweet treats. After all, what's a cake without frosting, or a brownie without a dollop of nut butter on top?

CHAPTER 1

*

MY SIMPLE STAPLES

Moo've over to plant-based milks

For people like myself who have ditched the dairy, it can be difficult to find plant-based alternatives to milk that aren't either costly or full of unfamiliar ingredients. Luckily, it's not only easy but also a lot less expensive to get milking at home. Oat milk is the easiest and cheapest as it requires no soaking—it's basically instant milk!

A number of my recipes feature almond milk, so can make your own instead of using the store-bought variety. But if you want a nut-free option or you don't like almonds, you can simply replace it with either plain oat milk or plain cashew milk. I've also given flavored versions of the latter two milks, as the creaminess of cashews works really well with chocolaty flavors and the bitterness of matcha green tea powder nicely offsets the sweetness of oat milk.

For an ultimately smooth result, you will need a high-speed blender, along with a nut milk bag (which you can buy super cheaply online, but if you are really stuck, just use a sieve; the milk won't be quite as smooth, but is perfectly fine for using in baking).

Homemade nut or oat milk is best stored in an airtight jar or bottle and should last for up to three days in the fridge (give it a good old shake before you use it). Reusing old glass containers also means avoiding waste in throwing away used cartons or boxes.

CLASSIC ALMOND
✳ MAKES 1 LARGE BOTTLE

1 cup whole unblanched almonds
4 cups cold water
1 Medjool date, pitted (optional)
pinch of Himalayan pink salt (optional)

1. Place the almonds in a bowl, cover with hot water and leave to soak for 2 hours. Drain, wash under cold water and drain again. Whizz all the ingredients in a high-speed blender for 2 minutes until totally smooth.

2. Strain the nut mixture through a nut bag into a clean airtight jar or bottle, and store in the fridge.

PLAIN OR CHCOLATE CASHEW ✳ MAKES 1 LARGE BOTTLE

1 cup cashew nuts
3½ cups water
2 tablespoons cacao powder (optional)
3 Medjool dates, pitted
pinch of Himalayan pink salt

1. Soak the cashews for 4 hours. Drain, then wash under cold water and drain again. Whizz all the ingredients in a high-speed blender for 2–3 minutes until smooth. Omit the cacao if preferred.

2. Pour into a clean airtight jar or bottle and store in the fridge.

PLAIN OR MATCHA OAT ✳ MAKES 1 LARGE BOTTLE

1 cup gluten-free rolled oats
3 cups water
½ teaspoon matcha green tea powder (optional)
1 Medjool date, pitted

1. Whizz all the ingredients in a high-speed blender for about 2–3 minutes until smooth. Alternatively, you can omit the matcha for a plain version.

2. Strain the nut mixture through a nut bag into a clean airtight jar or bottle, and store in the fridge.

✳ TOP TIP
Instead of throwing away the pulp, after straining, save it in an airtight container to use in baking—check out the Cinnamon, Oat, and Raisin Cookies on page 81.

Nuts about nut butter

Nut butters are a serious staple for me: used in smoothies and baking, dolloped onto porridge or even just eaten on the rocks, out of the jar, with a big old spoon. I love making my own, as they taste so much better and are a lot cheaper too.

Without professional equipment (and ingredients like palm oil), it's not easy to get homemade nut butters quite as smooth as some supermarket versions. However, roasting your nuts beforehand brings out their natural oils, which in turn helps them blend more easily.

Making nut butters does require patience—in the first few minutes of processing, a fine crumbly flour forms, which isn't something you'd want to smear on your morning banana bread. But have faith: keep processing for a few more minutes, and it will turn into the amazing nut butter you were hoping for. It will last for a good few weeks in the fridge; if it separates, juts give it a good old shake. Here I've narrowed it down to my all-time top nut butters.

HAZELNUT-CHOCOLATE SPREAD

The famous Italian version was invented to make chocolate (which was rationed at the time) go further by combining it with hazelnuts. Which is pretty ironic, as I need to ration myself when I make this or it will be gone before you can say "at least spread it on something first, woman." Everyone's favorite store-bought brand is pretty sugary and a bit ingredient-heavy for my liking, so I've given it a little Mrs. H makeover.

✳ MAKES 1 MEDIUM JAR

2 cups whole hazelnuts
7 tablespoons pure maple syrup
6 tablespoons cacao powder
pinch of Himalayan pink salt (optional)
½ cup almond milk (see page 18),
   or more if needed

1. Preheat the oven to 350°F. Spread the hazelnuts out evenly on a baking sheet. Roast for 6 to 8 minutes, removing the baking sheet halfway through to stir them around, or until golden (keep an eye on them to make sure they don't burn!).

2. Let them cool for a couple of minutes, then process in a food processor for 7 to 8 minutes, until they have the consistency of a gritty nut butter, stopping every few minutes to scrape down the sides of the bowl.

3. Add the maple syrup, cacao powder, and salt (if using) and process for 2 to 3 minutes more, until well combined and smooth. With the processor running, add the almond milk a tablespoon at a time until you have a velvety consistency. Spoon into a clean airtight jar and store in the fridge for up to a week.

SALTED PEANUT BUTTER

To me, peanut butter is the original. The founding member and don of the nut butters. PB and I have been going strong since my early teens (although perhaps in less healthy guises back then) and have shared many happy memories together since. Mr. H is also a superfan, as is Baby H, who has recently started asking me to put it on her dinner. A step too far perhaps, even for me!

✳ MAKES 1 MEDIUM JAR

2 cups raw blanched peanuts
pinch of Himalayan pink salt, or more to taste
1 tablespoon pure maple syrup,
    or more to taste (optional)

1. Preheat the oven to 350°F. Spread the peanuts out evenly on a baking sheet. Roast for about 15 minutes, or until golden, removing the baking sheet every 5 minutes or so to stir them around. Let them cool for about 10 minutes.

2. While the nuts are still warm, process them in a food processor for about 1 minute, or until they form a crumbly flour, then use a spatula to scrape down the mixture from the sides of the bowl. Process for a minute more, then scrape the mixture down again. It should start getting a bit lumpy at this point, but after one more round of processing, it should begin to transform into a smooth (albeit thick) nut butter.

3. Add the salt and the maple syrup (if using) and process for a final 5 to 7 minutes (depending on the strength of your machine), until the nut butter thins out and reaches the desired consistency. We are talking runny, creamy, and smooth here, people. Taste and more salt and maple syrup if needed, then spoon into a clean airtight jar and store in the fridge for up to a week.

MAPLE-CINNAMON CASHEW BUTTER

I use cashew butter a lot in my baking, as it's so creamy and milky. I also use it to make "milk" chocolate and salted caramel, and to add gooeyness to my brownies (see page 53). Cashew butter is also delicious in its own right, and my favorite way to eat it is dolloped onto banana bread with a little maple syrup and cinnamon. That combination is what inspired this recipe, as the flavors just work so well together.

* MAKES 1 MEDIUM JAR

2 cups raw cashews
1 tablespoon pure maple syrup
1 tablespoon ground cinnamon
pinch of Himalayan pink salt (optional)

1. Preheat the oven to 325°F. Spread the cashews out evenly on a baking sheet. Roast for about 15 minutes, until pale golden, removing the baking sheet every 5 minutes or so to stir them around.

2. Let cool until cool enough to handle, then process in a food processor for about 8 minutes, or until creamy, stopping every few minutes to scrape down the sides of the bowl.

3. Transfer the nut butter to a mixing bowl, add the maple syrup, cinnamon, and salt (if using), and stir until all the ingredients are well mixed. Spoon into a clean airtight jar and store in the fridge for up to a week.

*TOP TIP

For plain cashew butter to bake (or unbake) with, just leave out the maple syrup and cinnamon. Or if you fancy giving it a festive twist, swap out the cinnamon for a mix of ground spices.

COCONUT-VANILLA ALMOND BUTTER

If almond butter went on holiday to the Caribbean, got a sun tan, and drank one too many cocktails, then this is what it would taste like. We are talking golden, nutty, and smooth, with a tropical twist and a sweet vanilla kick. Sweet vs. salty, nutty vs. fruity, this nut butter is the one bringing all the sass. It's also a little cheaper per spoonful than other nut butters to make, as coconut tends to be a lot less expensive than nuts as ingredients go. What's not to like? * MAKES 1 MEDIUM JAR

2 cups whole almonds
1 cup desiccated coconut
2 tablespoons coconut oil, melted
½ teaspoon pure vanilla extract

1. Preheat the oven to 350°F. Spread the almonds out evenly on a baking sheet. Roast for 10 minutes, or until starting to brown, removing the baking sheet halfway through to stir them around.

2. Remove from the oven, spread the coconut evenly over the baking sheet, and bake for 2 minutes more.

3. Let cool until cool enough to handle, then process in a food processor for 2 minutes to break down the almonds.

4. Add the melted coconut oil and vanilla and process for 10 to 12 minutes more, until a smooth, buttery consistency is reached, stopping every few minutes to scrape down the sides of the bowl. Spoon into a clean airtight jar and store in the fridge for up to a week.

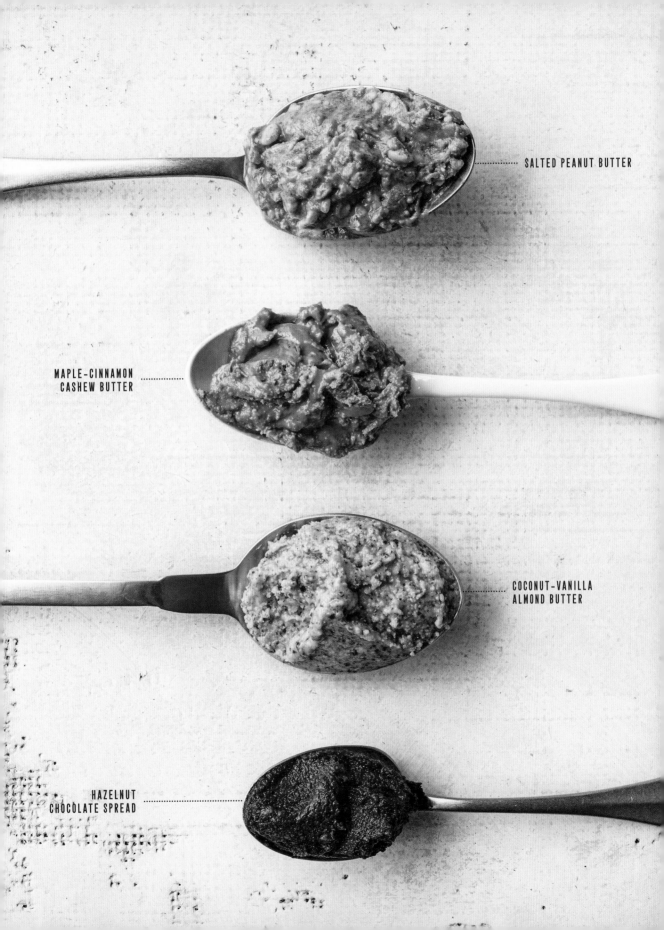

SALTED PEANUT BUTTER

MAPLE-CINNAMON
CASHEW BUTTER

COCONUT-VANILLA
ALMOND BUTTER

HAZELNUT
CHOCOLATE SPREAD

FOUR-INGREDIENT CHOCOLATE FROSTING

When I was younger, my mom used to make us the most incredible birthday cakes. They were so chocolaty and moist, but without a doubt the best bit was the frosting—chocolate buttercream. I would go so far as saying that it was my favorite food then. My dairy-free re-creation is just as chocolaty, creamy, and delicious, but features only four ingredients. It's a one-bowl wonder that doesn't involve any blending, just a whole lot of spoon-licking.

❋ MAKES ENOUGH TO FROST 1 CAKE (BUT DOUBLE UP IF YOU ALSO WANT TO USE IT FOR FILLING THE CAKE, TOO)

¼ cup chilled full-fat coconut milk (see page 12)
2 tablespoons pure maple syrup
1 tablespoon cacao powder
1 tablespoon peanut butter
 (see page 21)

1. Simply combine all the ingredients in a mixing bowl and stir together well until smooth and creamy.

2. Spread over your cake/brownies/other half and enjoy! Use immediately or store in the fridge for up to one day.

CREAM "CHEESE" FROSTING

Think you can't have cream cheese frosting without the dairy? Think again, my friends! Red Velvet Cake (page 149) just wouldn't be the same without it, and it goes fantastically with other cakes too, but luckily I have a secret weapon up my sleeve. It actually comes in a tub rather than from my sleeve, and it's called nutritional yeast. Don't be put off by the not-so-appetizing name; it's a total game-changer when it comes to making "cheesy" flavors. It's deactivated, so it won't make bakes rise like normal yeast does, and it's usually available as flakes. Blended with a few other natural ingredients, it gives the perfect hint of cheesiness to this frosting.

❋ MAKES ENOUGH TO FROST 1 CAKE

1 cup raw cashews, soaked in water
 for at least 4 hours, then drained
1 cup chilled full-fat coconut milk (see page 12)
1 to 2 tablespoons fresh lemon juice
½ cup coconut oil
¼ cup pure maple syrup
1 tablespoon nutritional yeast
1 teaspoon pure vanilla extract

1. Process all the ingredients in a food processor for about 10 minutes, or until super smooth and creamy, stopping every couple of minutes to scrape down the sides of the bowl.

2. Place in the fridge for an hour to set (otherwise, it will be too liquid to pipe onto anything), then spoon into a piping bag and frost away! Use immediately or store in the fridge for up to one day.

THE CHOCOLATE SAUCE OF DREAMS

Friday lunchtimes were a time of sheer excitement at my school, as that was when the cafeteria made their famous chocolate cake with chocolate sauce. If you didn't get there soon after the lunch bell rang, all that would be left for dessert was Jell-O. For me, therefore, chocolate sauce is not only delicious but wonderfully nostalgic.

This sauce is incredibly simple to make, and it complements just about any dessert (or snack, or breakfast) under the sun. Who doesn't love a warm, chocolaty drizzle over their dessert? * MAKES ABOUT 1 CUP

6 tablespoons coconut oil
6 tablespoons cacao powder
¼ cup pure maple syrup
2 tablespoons full-fat coconut milk,
  chilled (see page 12)

1. Melt the coconut oil in a heatproof bowl over a saucepan half-full of gently boiling water over medium heat, then stir in the other ingredients until you have a smooth, glossy chocolate sauce.

2. Serve right away, or, if you want it a little thicker, place it in the fridge for a few minutes to harden up.

3. Store any leftovers in an airtight container in the fridge for up to a week or freeze for up to 2 months. To reuse, reheat gently as above or on the lowest temperature in your oven.

*TOP TIP
For an insanely good hot chocolate drink, add your milk of choice to the sauce and heat in a pan.

CHOCOLATE MOUSSE

For most people, avocado isn't really what comes to mind when they think of chocolate mousse. Which is why I don't tell people the secret ingredient in mine until after they have tried it. I've had many a dinner party where I've served it up to unsuspecting guests who have later left my house with a very happy tummy and a new chocolate mousse recipe scribbled down on a bit of paper.

This nifty little mousse is amazing on its own, but you can also use it as a tart or pie filling, or spoon it over berries for the ultimate in delicious breakfasts. It's a great way to use up any ripe avocados lurking in your fruit bowl! * SERVES 1

½ ripe avocado, pitted and peeled
3 Medjool dates, pitted
¼ cup chilled full-fat coconut milk (see page 12)
3 tablespoons cacao powder
2 tablespoons coconut oil

Process all the ingredients in a food processor for about 5 minutes, or until a silky-smooth mousse forms, stopping every minute or so to scrape down the sides of the bowl to ensure it is all blended evenly. Serve immediately.

COCONUT WHIPPED CREAM

Whipped cream popped up in my childhood on exciting occasions: as a pancake topping on Shrove Tuesday, on top of creamy hot chocolates to warm us up on Fireworks Night, and sometimes, when my mom wasn't looking, it squirted itself directly into our little mouths. It's the perfect finishing touch to pies, tarts, trifles (if you are having an '80s throwback party), and fruit salad, too.

This recipe came about when I was having people over for dinner but was so busy that I hadn't had time to make anything for dessert. I had a bunch of avocados hanging out in my fruit bowl, so I made my chocolate mousse (see page 25), and to make it look a little fancy, I whipped up some coconut milk, piped it on top, and finished it with cacao nibs and goji berries. My friends thought it had taken me ages to make . . . little did they know!

* MAKES ENOUGH TO COVER 1 CAKE

1 (14-ounce) can full-fat coconut milk
2 tablespoons pure maple syrup
½ teaspoon pure vanilla extract

1. Place the can of coconut milk in the fridge overnight to harden up (see page 12).

2. Spoon the solid white coconut cream from the can into a mixing bowl (save the clear liquid for another use), add the maple syrup and vanilla, and beat with a handheld mixer for about a minute, or until it becomes light and fluffy. Spoon or pipe onto your favorite dessert and enjoy.

BERRY CHIA JELLY

Jelly really takes me back to being little: jelly sandwiches for tea, a spoonful of jelly stirred into hot rice pudding, my mom's incredible cake filled with jelly that my brother and I simply referred to as "jelly cake," my grandma's amazing homemade jelly tarts . . .

I tend to stay away from traditional store-bought jelly due to its insanely high sugar content, but I still love the stuff, so of course I make my own. It's ridiculously easy to make, and it tastes just as good (if not better). * MAKES 1 MEDIUM JAR

about 1 cup hulled strawberries
    or raspberries
2 tablespoons chia seeds
2 tablespoons pure maple syrup
¼ cup water

1. Blend all the ingredients in a blender for a minute or so, until they form a smooth liquid.

2. Pour the mixture into a small saucepan and heat over medium heat until it starts to boil. Reduce the heat to low and cook, stirring, for about 20 minutes, or until it starts to thicken.

3. Let the jelly cool and then pop it into a clean airtight jar and store in the fridge for up to 5 days or freeze in an airtight freezerproof container for up to one month.

* TOP TIP
If you want to make this look how it does when it comes out of the spray can, just pop it into a piping bag fitted with an open star tip and pipe away!

Salted caramel, two ways

I love the combination of sweet plus salty so much that I couldn't decide which salted caramel recipe to share with you guys: the sticky-gooey date one that I sandwich between cookies or spoon onto apples, or the runny-smooth sauce that's the best drizzled over, well, anything. So you've got both. The only tough bit now is deciding which one to make first.

STICKY SALTED DATE CARAMEL * MAKES 1 MEDIUM JAR

3 tablespoons coconut oil
5 Medjool dates, pitted
6 tablespoons cashew butter (see tip, page 22)
pinch of Himalayan pink salt

1. Process all the ingredients in a food processor or high-speed blender for about 5 minutes, or until smooth, stopping every minute or so to scrape down the sides of the bowl or blender jar.

2. Use right away or store in an airtight container in the fridge for up to a week or freeze for up to 2 months.

SALTED CARAMEL SAUCE * MAKES 1 MEDIUM JAR

NUT FREE

½ cup pure maple syrup
½ cup full-fat coconut milk
pinch of Himalayan pink salt

1. Heat a saucepan over medium heat, then add the maple syrup and cook until it starts to bubble.

2. Add the coconut milk and salt and stir in gently, then boil for 15 minutes more, stirring regularly, until it begins to thicken and darken in color.

3. Remove the pan from the heat and let cool. Use right away or store in an airtight container in the fridge for up to a week or freeze for up to 2 months.

> *TOP TIP
> If you have extra caramel, pour it into ice cube trays and freeze it. It lasts for months, and you can just defrost what you need when you need it!

THREE-INGREDIENT INSTANT DOUBLE CHOCOLATE NICE CREAM

NUT FREE

Time flies when you're having fun. Time goes very slowly, however, when you're waiting for ice cream to set. However, if you remember to pop a couple of chopped-up bananas in the freezer the night before, then you've got it covered.

I got into making this after we took a little trip with Baby H to Italy just before her first birthday and she discovered her love of ice cream. When we came home I didn't want to deny her, so I made her this, and she never noticed the difference. I actually made it for us all for breakfast on her birthday, and the photos of my happy ice cream–covered birthday baby girl are something I'll treasure forever. ✳ SERVES 2

2 ripe bananas, peeled, chopped into chunks, and frozen overnight
2 tablespoons cacao powder
2 tablespoons cacao nibs

1. Blend the bananas and cacao powder in a high-speed blender for 30 seconds to 1 minute, until they have the texture of soft-serve ice cream. Stir in the cacao nibs, spoon into bowls, and demolish!

A SUNDAE WELL SPENT . . . VANILLA CASHEW ICE CREAM

When Mr. H and I were on our honeymoon, or rather our "maple-moon" (honey ain't vegan, folks), we went to an incredible plant-based Mexican restaurant in LA. It was my birthday and Mr. H pretended to go to the bathroom so that he could ask them for a special dessert. What they served blew my mind: crunchy cookies with ice cream that tasted just like, well, ice cream! As soon as we got home I set about re-creating it, and this is just the ticket. ✳ SERVES 2

1½ cups raw cashews, soaked in
    water for 4 hours, then drained
1 cup chilled full-fat coconut milk (see page 12)
1½ cups pure maple syrup
1 teaspoon pure vanilla extract

TOPPINGS (OPTIONAL)
The Chocolate Sauce of Dreams (page 25)
sliced bananas and strawberries
nut butters (see pages 20–22)

1. Process the cashews, coconut milk, maple syrup, and vanilla in a food processor for about 5 minutes, or until smooth and runny.

2. Pour into a freezerproof container and freeze for about 4 hours, or until set, taking it out every hour or so and giving it a stir, if possible, so that it freezes evenly. It will keep in the freezer for about a month.

3. To serve, take the ice cream out of the freezer an hour beforehand to soften up. Add your desired toppings just before serving—the more, the better!

✳TOP TIP
You can use this as an ice cream base and mix it up using all sorts of different flavors. I love adding frozen berries, pecans, and a little cinnamon or just some good old-fashioned cacao powder.

Raw chocolate

When I was little my parents used to say that my pocket money "burned a hole in my pocket," which I never understood, but I now know that it means I spent it rather quickly, mostly on chocolate. These days, chocolate burns a hole in my fridge.

Making chocolate is pretty simple, basically involving just an oil and some cacao powder, although most people like to add a little sweetness, and some prefer their chocolate on the milkier, creamier side, both doable by throwing in a couple of extra ingredients. All three types use the same method though—what could be easier?!

You may have been scared to make chocolate after hearing fancy words like "chocolatier" and "tempering," but I promise you it's not complicated at all. Tempering chocolate doesn't mean making your chocolate grumpy; it just means heating and cooling it slowly so that it's glossy and smooth once it sets. There are expensive machines that do this, or special thermometers to fool around with, but in my experience all you need to do is to give your chocolate a good stir before you use it and then let it cool before you refrigerate it.

I like to use cacao butter when making white or "milk" chocolate and coconut oil for dark chocolate (see page 12 for more on this), but whichever one you use, I promise you it will be delicious!

WHITE CHOCOLATE

½ cup cacao butter
¼ cup cashew butter (see tip, page 22)
3 tablespoons pure maple syrup
¼ teaspoon pure vanilla extract
pinch of Himalayan pink salt

MILK CHOCOLATE

½ cup cacao butter
¼ cup cacao powder
¼ cup pure maple syrup
2 tablespoons cashew butter (see tip, page 22)
pinch of Himalayan pink salt

DARK CHOCOLATE

½ cup coconut oil
¼ cup cacao powder
2 tablespoons pure maple syrup
pinch of Himalayan pink salt

1. Melt the cacao butter or coconut oil in a heatproof bowl over a saucepan half-full of gently boiling water over medium heat until about 80 percent melted, then remove from the heat and stir quickly to melt the remainder. (This should stop it from getting too hot.) Stir in the other ingredients until you have a smooth and glossy chocolate mixture.

2. Let cool for 5 minutes or so, then pour the melted chocolate into a silicone chocolate mold, an ice cube tray, or mini paper cupcake liners and pop them into the fridge for about 15 minutes to set.

I have been a snack fiend since I started school at age five and a half (because the half is very important when you're small). When my mom used to collect me from school, she would have to bring me something sweet to tide me over until dinnertime, otherwise all hell would break loose. She later realized that I wasn't being intentionally grumpy but that I am a little hypoglycemic, which means that if I don't eat every couple of hours or so, my blood sugar drops and I get what is now commonly known as "hangry." So snacking is in my blood, quite literally.

I'm often out and about during the day, as I'm sure many of you are too, so I need to be prepared when it comes to healthy energy-boosting snacks. I go equipped with a backpack, known in our household as "the snackpack," to fit in all the provisions made from delicious natural ingredients we may need, at the same time saving myself from aching shoulders.

This chapter is snack-tion packed with all my absolute favorite balls, bites, and bars. These recipes are all designed so that you can make them very quickly and easily, with or without a small child attached to one hip. Now that's what I call smart snacking.

CHAPTER 2

*

GRAB-AND-GO BARS & BALLS

BLUEBERRY BREAKFAST BARS

For a lot of people, weekday mornings usually start like this: alarm goes off; snooze; snooze; snooze; *insert swear word* I need to wake up!; jump in the shower; throw on clothes; grab handbag/manbag/child, and run; get to the bus/train, sit down and breathe. It's at this point that your tummy starts growling so loudly that you wonder if the person behind you is in fact a lion escaped from the zoo. Everyone turns to look at you, and you realize you are really quite hungry. Sound familiar?

These breakfast flapjacks are one of my Sunday baking staples. They taste amazing and contain a bunch of fabulous ingredients to keep you going and tame that roaring lion in your tummy. Tasty, easy, healthy, and transportable—what's not to like! * MAKES 16 BARS

1 cup gluten-free rolled oats
1 ripe banana, peeled and mashed
½ cup blueberries
⅓ cup chopped toasted hazelnuts
3 tablespoons pure maple syrup
1 tablespoon coconut oil, melted
½ teaspoon ground cinnamon

1. Preheat the oven to 350°F.

2. Simply mix together all the ingredients in a mixing bowl. Tip the mixture into a shallow 8-inch square baking pan or a disposable aluminum pan (see page 48). Bake for 15 to 20 minutes, until the top is golden. Let cool.

3. Cut into 16 bars and store in an airtight container in the fridge for up to 5 days or in the freezer for up to a month. In the morning, just grab and go!

*TOP TIP
Buy strawberries when
they are in season and
freeze to use in later
months when only the
less-tasty (less-local)
varieties are available.

STRAWBERRY "CHEESECAKE" BALLS

Nothing beats British strawberries. Every year I look forward to the month of May with its two bank holidays, potentially a day or two of warmish weather, and the official beginning of the strawberry season. So when home-grown strawberries hit the shelves, I stock up and pop them on my morning pancakes, stick them in smoothies and salads, and chuck them into "cheesecake" balls.

These beauties require only four ingredients and taste just like strawberry cheesecake because of the creamy cashews and naturally sweet dates, with not a smidgen of cream cheese nor a cookie crumb in sight.

✳ MAKES ABOUT 12 BALLS

1 cup pitted Medjool dates
1 cup raw cashews
½ cup hulled strawberries
2 cups ground almonds
freeze-dried strawberries, crushed,
   for coating (optional)

1. Process the dates, cashews, and strawberries in a food processor until they form a thick paste.

2. Pour into a mixing bowl and stir in the ground almonds until well mixed.

3. Roll the mixture into about 12 balls and place in the fridge for an hour to firm up. Store in an airtight container in the fridge for up to 3 days or freeze for up to 2 months. Roll in crushed freeze-fried strawberries before serving, if desired.

APRICOT, CARROT, AND GINGER BALLS

I used to steer clear of dried apricots, as they were too leathery and chewy for my liking, until my lovely friend brought over some dried apricots from an organic, zero-waste grocery shop for me to try. These were different from any I had ever tasted (or seen) before; they weren't tough at all, had a wonderful hint of caramel to them, and were brown rather than orange. I did some research and it transpires that the orange color of some dried apricots is due to the sulfur dioxide added to them. That's not great for you, especially if you are asthmatic, so if you can source the organic unsulfured ones, it's well worth it.

The combination of juicy apricots with refreshing carrot and zesty ginger here makes these balls a winning formula.

✳ MAKES ABOUT 15 SMALL BALLS

½ cup sunflower seeds
1 cup pitted Medjool dates
½ cup desiccated coconut, plus extra
   for coating
1 cup dried apricots
½ cup grated carrot
1 teaspoon ground ginger

1. Grind the sunflower seeds in a food processor for 1 minute.

2. Add all the other ingredients and process for about 1 minute, or until they form a sticky mixture.

3. Roll the mixture into about 15 small balls, then roll in more coconut to coat. Store in an airtight container in the fridge for up to 5 days or freeze for up to 2 months.

COCONUT-CASHEW BALLS

I wanted to call this recipe "C bombs," but then I realized that that could potentially come across a little rude. I also thought all the ingredients began with the letter "C," but then I remembered about the dates.

These are my staple snack. They are chewy, coconutty, and chock-full of good ingredients. I consume them come eleven o'clock and sometimes again for an afternoon snack. The chia seeds make them crunchy, and the cranberries provide the perfect hit of tartness to complement the sweetness of the dates.

In summary, these balls are the classic companion to a coffee if you want to feel cozy on a cold day. They are non-chocolaty, too, which means that if I do choose to give a little chunk to my cutest, cheekiest comrade, there isn't quite so much cleaning up to do. How many Cs in that?

✳ MAKES ABOUT 16 BALLS

1 cup raw cashews
½ cup cashew butter (see tip, page 22)
½ cup desiccated coconut
2 tablespoons coconut oil
1½ cups pitted Medjool dates
2 tablespoons chia seeds
¼ cup dried cranberries

1. Process the cashews, cashew butter, coconut, coconut oil, and dates in a food processor for 2 to 3 minutes, until they form a sticky ball. Add the chia seeds and cranberries and pulse for a minute until they are mixed in.

2. Roll the mixture into about 16 balls and place in the fridge for an hour to firm up. Store in an airtight container in the fridge for up to 2 weeks or freeze for up to 2 months.

FIGGY FRUITCAKE BALLS

Don't get me wrong, I love dates like they're going out of fashion (as if), but it's nice sometimes to experiment with different flavors. I adore fresh figs in the summer, and the dried ones make me feel all festive come wintertime.

One of my favorite ways to eat dried figs is these fruitcake balls. They remind me of my wedding cake; each of the layers was a different flavor, with a fruitcake layer as the base. These balls are a) a lot quicker to make than a wedding cake, trust me, and b) just as delicious as a wedding cake. They make a wonderful snack all year round and are great if you don't like dates or are looking for a slightly cheaper alternative.

✳ MAKES ABOUT 15 BALLS

1 cup dried figs
1 cup whole almonds
finely grated zest of ½ orange
1 teaspoon pumpkin pie spice
⅓ cup raisins
¼ cup dried cranberries

1. Process the figs, almonds, orange zest and spice in a food processor for about a minute, or until you have a sticky mixture.

2. Add the raisins and cranberries and pulse for 30 seconds, or until they are mixed in.

3. Roll the mixture into about 15 balls and store in an airtight container in the fridge for up to 2 weeks or freeze for up to 2 months.

✳ **TOP TIP**
To make these into festive Christmas balls, spoon a little coconut milk on top and add a few goji berries or dried cranberries and a mint leaf or two.

CHOCOLATE-ORANGE BALLS

When I was a little girl, my grandpa used to have a magical orange tree. All year round it would stand in his lounge producing oranges never bigger than a golf ball. But amazingly, once they fell off the tree, they would turn into Terry's Chocolate Oranges (or so he told us), packaging and all. Now, we never actually saw this happen, but my brother, cousins, and I always took Grandpa's word for it. Even after the truth came out, the tree still continued to produce its "fruit" on birthdays and other special occasions. A few years back shortly after Mr. H and I moved into the house we had bought together, before my beloved grandpa passed away, a little orange tree turned up on our doorstep as a housewarming present.

Mine is a chocolate-orange tree 2.0, as it produces these four-ingredient chocolate orange balls. OK, so maybe you're not as gullible as I once was, but you can believe me when I say these balls are just as good as the original. ✳ MAKES ABOUT 10 SMALL BALLS

1 cup raw cashews
1 cup pitted Medjool dates
¼ cup cacao powder
finely grated zest of ½ orange

1. Process the cashews in a food processor for 30 seconds, then add the other ingredients and process until mixed together well.

2. Roll the mixture into about 10 small balls and store in an airtight container in the fridge for up to 2 weeks or freeze for up to 2 months.

PEANUT BUTTER CRUNCH BALLS

I'm not a sporty person (far from it), but I absolutely love running. It feels so freeing to be outside in the open air running as fast as my little (and short—thanks, Dad) legs will carry me. When Baby H was small and I wanted to do some exercise, I would pop her in the stroller and get my jog on. It was so lovely, and a great way to get her to sleep, too.

Before I set off on my little runs, I would always have a couple of these balls to give me energy and keep me going. Peanut butter is packed with protein, good fats and fiber, so it gives you a slow and steady release of energy, and also fills you up. Of course, it also tastes totally delicious, so whether you are a long distance runner or more of a "walk to the fridge" kind of exerciser, these are the snack for you! ✳ MAKES ABOUT 15 BALLS

1 cup peanut butter (see page 21)
½ teaspoon Himalayan pink salt
2 cups pitted Medjool dates
1 cup raw blanched peanuts, toasted (see page 21)
¼ cup cacao nibs

1. Process the peanut butter, salt, and dates in a food processor for 1 minute, or until they form a sticky paste.

2. Add the peanuts and pulse for 30 seconds to 1 minute, depending on how chunky you want them to be. Add the cacao nibs and pulse for 10 seconds more.

3. Roll the mixture into about 15 balls and store in an airtight container in the fridge for up to 2 weeks or freeze for up to 2 months.

CINNAMON-APPLE GRANOLA BARS

In celebration of me turning old (thirty, eek), we went on a lovely weekend trip to Verona. It turns out travelling with a baby is much easier before they start a) crawling and b) eating, but while there's not much you can do about the former apart from being in party entertainer mode for the duration of the flight, the latter can be helped by careful planning and a whole backpack of snacks (the "snackpack").

I had some apples that needed using up and I wanted to make something we could take with us that was only made with natural ingredients. Cue these bad boys. They taste pretty damn delicious, and are so handy on the go. * MAKES 16 BARS

    2 apples, any variety, quartered and cored
    8 Medjool dates, pitted
    ½ cup cashew butter (see tip, page 22)
    ½ cup almond milk (see page 18)
    2 cups gluten-free rolled oats
    3 tablespoons ground flaxseeds
    1 tablespoon ground cinnamon

1. Preheat the oven to 350°F. Line a shallow 8-inch square baking pan with parchment paper, or use a disposable aluminum pan (see page 48).

2. Process the apples, dates, cashew butter, and almond milk in a blender or food processor until you have a smooth puree. Pour into a mixing bowl and fold in the oats, ground flaxseeds, and cinnamon until well combined.

3. Spoon the mixture into the prepared pan and press down with the back of the spoon. Bake for 30 minutes. Let cool.

4. Cut into 16 bars. Store in an airtight container in the fridge for up to a week or freeze for up to 2 months.

BANOFFEE BARS

We go through a lot of bananas in our household, which perhaps explains why Baby H is such a cheeky monkey. Every morning we have smoothies (with banana), porridge (with banana) and quite often pancakes (with, you guessed it, banana). But it's hard sometimes to estimate quite how many we need for the week, and with bananas I always like to plan ahead to give them time to ripen. When I have a surplus of bananas in my fruit bowl, there is always a way to use them up. If I'm in need of some easy snacks, I make these. The bananas help bind everything together—the proverbial glue. And like a very sticky glue, these are super. * MAKES 16 BARS

    2 ripe bananas, peeled
    3 tablespoons coconut oil, melted
    2 tablespoons pure maple syrup
    1 chia seed "egg" (see page 13)
    2 cups gluten-free rolled oats
    pinch of Himalayan pink salt

1. Preheat the oven to 350°F. Line a shallow 8-inch square baking pan with parchment paper, or use a disposable aluminum pan (see page 48).

2. Mash the bananas in a mixing bowl. Add the coconut oil, maple syrup, and chia seed "egg" and stir together. Add the oats and the salt and stir until the oats are evenly covered with the banana mixture.

3. Spoon the mixture into the prepared pan and press down evenly with the back of the spoon. Bake for 20 minutes, or until it starts to look a little golden on top. Let cool.

4. Cut into 16 bars. Store in an airtight container in the fridge for up to a week or freeze for up to 2 months.

STICKY DATE SLICES

One Sunday evening in the Hollingsworth household the unthinkable happened. We ran out of oats. Panic began to strike. How would we survive? The shops were closed and my online order wasn't coming until the next day. But then I remembered—puffed rice.

I pulled myself together and got my head back in the game. What a wonderful opportunity to create something new, I thought, although it's always touch and go as to whether Baby H will like the new things I give her to try. Luckily, this recipe passed the test and is now a firm favorite in our house. Think crispy puffed rice with a sticky caramelly date mixture, juicy raisins and crunchy almond flakes. ✳ MAKES 16 SLICES

1 cup pitted Medjool dates
½ cup peanut butter (see page 21)
¼ cup coconut oil
pinch of Himalayan pink salt
3 cups puffed brown rice
½ cup slivered almonds
½ cup raisins

1. Line a shallow 8-inch square baking pan with parchment paper, or use a disposable aluminum pan (see page 48).

2. Blend the dates, peanut butter, coconut oil, and salt in a blender until you have a sticky caramel. Pour the mixture into a mixing bowl and stir in the puffed rice, almonds, and raisins.

3. Spoon the mixture into the prepared pan, then press down evenly with the back of the spoon. Freeze for 1 hour, or until set.

4. Cut into 16 slices and store in an airtight container in the fridge for up to a week or freeze for up to 2 months.

PUFFED RICE SLABS

Rice crispy cakes are easy, kid-friendly baking and the ultimate childhood throwback for us adults. A lot of our childhood nostalgia—the toys, clothes and lack of social media—will seem alien to adults of the future. But I hope that easy, messy, chocolaty baking, where licking the spoon/bowl/your fingers is a must, makes its way down to generation touchscreen.

These days, however, there are so many allergies, dietary requirements and intolerances that the rice crispy cake recipes of old just won't cut the mustard for many. I've done a little tweaking and come up with an even better version. Now there is no excuse—whether old or young, these are calling your name. Let's make sure the magic of chocolaty puffed rice deliciousness gets passed down to our little ones so that one day they can pass it down to theirs. How's that for a legacy! ✳ MAKES 16 SLABS

½ cup peanut butter (see page 21)
½ cup pure maple syrup
¼ cup coconut oil, melted
¼ cup cacao powder
3 cups puffed brown rice

1. Line a shallow 8-inch square baking pan with parchment paper, or use a disposable aluminum pan (see page 48).

2. Stir together the peanut butter, maple syrup, coconut oil, and cacao powder in a mixing bowl until smooth. Add the puffed rice and mix well.

3. Spoon the mixture into the prepared pan and press down evenly with the back of the spoon. Refrigerate for a couple of hours to set. Cut into 16 slabs and store in an airtight container in a cool, dark place for up to 5 days.

✳ TOP TIP
For a nut-free alternative,
replace the peanut butter
with tahini.

CHOC CHIP NO-COOK COOKIE DOUGH SLABS

Confession time. Put your hand up if you used to eat most of the cookie dough before it even made it into the oven. Put your other hand up if you have ever dug all the chunks out of cookie dough ice cream, leaving behind a tub of melty vanilla. If you are either or both of the above, then you're in luck. These slabs require no baking and there is no need to forage around with a spoon for them either.

While baked cookies still hold a special place in my heart, there is just something about chewy raw cookie dough that totally hits the spot. Add some chocolate chips and you've got something really special going on. ✱ MAKES 16 SLABS

1½ cups gluten-free rolled oats
1 cup ground almonds
pinch of Himalayan pink salt
½ cup pure maple syrup
6 tablespoons coconut oil, melted
⅓ cup cashew butter (see tip, page 22)
½ teaspoon pure vanilla extract
½ cup small chunks raw chocolate (whatever variety you prefer; see page 31), plus more for topping, if desired

1. Line a shallow 8-inch square baking pan with parchment paper, or use a disposable aluminum pan (see page 48).

2. Process the oats in a food processor or high-speed blender for about 30 seconds until they form a flour. Transferto a mixing bowl, add the ground almonds and salt, and stir together. Add the wet ingredients and mix well. Finally, stir in the chocolate chunks.

3. Transfer the mixture to the prepared pan, then press down evenly with the back of a spoon. Place in the freezer for 2 hours to set.

4. If you want to make an even more chocolaty slab, place ¼ cup chopped raw chocolate in a heatproof bowl over a saucepan half-full of gently boiling water over medium heat and stir until it melts, then drizzle the melted chocolate over the cookie dough. Return to the freezer for 15 minutes to set, then cut into 16 slabs. Store in an airtight container in the fridge for up to a week or freeze for up to 2 months.

PB & J (THE RELATIONSHIP THAT WILL NEVER) CRUMBLE SANDWICHES

I thought BP & J would last forever (that's Brad Pitt & Jen), felt sure that Gwyneth and Chris would never "uncouple," and the thought of Ryan Gosling and Amy Adams parting ways just broke my heart. I've heard rumors that even fish and chips are on the brink, something to do with tofu muscling in while fish was off swimming (he was battered apparently). But peanut butter and jelly (or jam as our friends across the pond say)? Nothing can come between those two. Oh sure, jelly flirts with coconut milk, and peanut butter makes a good chocolate companion, but there is something about the nutty and fruity, salty and sweet combination that is unparalleled in its amazingness. I guess opposites really do attract.

These crumble sandwiches are something else. For most people, a sandwich would contain bread, but bread is kinda not my jam, so wholemeal out, crumble in. Think gooey, sticky PB & J sandwiches inside crunchy, oaty crumble—sounds perfect, right? * MAKES 16 SQUARES

FOR THE CRUMBLE
4 cups gluten-free rolled oats
1 ripe large banana, peeled and mashed
½ cup plus 2 tablespoons pure maple syrup
6 tablespoons coconut oil, melted
6 tablespoons peanut butter (see page 21)
pinch of Himalayan pink salt

FOR THE FILLING
½ cup peanut butter (see page 21)
Berry Chia Jelly (page 26, made with raspberries)

1. Preheat the oven to 350°F. Line a shallow 8-inch square baking pan with parchment paper, or use a disposable aluminum pan (see page 48).

2. To make the crumble, stir together the oats, banana, half the maple syrup, and half the melted coconut oil in a mixing bowl until well mixed. Spread out on a baking sheet and bake for 10 minutes.

3. Meanwhile, mix the peanut butter with the remaining maple syrup and melted coconut oil in a separate mixing bowl until it forms a smooth liquid.

4. Once the crumble has finished baking, add it to the bowl with the peanut butter mixture and mix well. Spoon half the crumble mixture into the prepared pan and press down evenly with the back of the spoon.

5. To make the filling, spoon the peanut butter on top of the crumble and smooth with a spatula so that it covers the crumble evenly. Repeat with the jelly, then spoon the remaining crumble mixture over the top. Bake for 20 minutes, then let cool. Place in the fridge for 1 hour to set.

6. Cut into 16 squares. Store in an airtight container in the fridge for up to 5 days or freeze for up to 2 months.

I love a traybake. For me, they are the ultimate in hassle-free cooking: minimal mess, minimal cleanup, maximum taste. In short, winning. I would say that the recipes in this chapter are easy as pie, but I actually think they're even easier than that. They are also all ridiculously easy to eat; we're talking fudgy brownies, melt-in-the mouth chocolate fudge flapjacks, fruity crumbles, and so much more. These are some of my own all-time favorite recipes, but they're also perfect for sharing with friends, family, and colleagues.

For the "trays" in my "traybakes," I tend to use 8-inch square aluminum foil pans, which I totally rate because they are 1) recyclable, 2) easy to transport, and 3) cleanup-free. However, it's fine to use a shallow 8-inch square baking pan lined with parchment paper or even a silicone mold instead. If your pan is bigger or smaller than mine, simply scale the recipe up or down accordingly.

I'm so excited to share these dairy-, gluten-, and refined sugar–free traybakes with you, so that you, in turn, can share them with everyone you know and love.

CHAPTER 3

*

TRÈS EASY TRAYBAKES

NO-BAKE SALTED CARAMEL OR CHOCOLATE FUDGE FLAPJACKS

The day I created this recipe, it was a scorching-hot day in London. I had been brainstorming about fudge-covered raisin flapjacks and was really happy with my mixture, but I couldn't face going anywhere near the oven to bake it, as it was just too hot. So I made a couple of tweaks and the result was these insane no-bake versions.

These are one of the best sweet treats I've ever created, selling out every week everywhere I've supplied them, and I've taught hundreds of people how to make these at my baking classes, with rave reviews. The best thing about this recipe is that you can either make them chocolaty, or leave out the cacao powder for a salted caramel fudge (or, my personal favorite, make a little bit of both and marble them together.) ✳ MAKES 16 FLAPJACKS

FOR THE FLAPJACKS
⅓ cup coconut oil, melted
⅓ cup cashew butter (see tip, page 22), or any other nut or seed butter
¼ cup pure maple syrup
2 cups gluten-free rolled oats
⅓ cup raisins

FOR THE FUDGE
½ cup cacao powder (optional—omit if you want a salted caramel fudge)
½ cup pure maple syrup
¼ cup cashew butter (see tip, page 22), or any other nut or seed butter
½ cup coconut oil, melted
pinch of Himalayan pink salt

1. Line a shallow 8-inch square baking pan with parchment paper, or use a disposable aluminum pan (see page 48).

2. To make the flapjacks, stir together the melted coconut oil, cashew butter, and maple syrup in a mixing bowl until well mixed, then stir in the oats and raisins.

3. Spoon the mixture into the prepared pan, then press down evenly with the back of the spoon. Place in the fridge while you make the fudge.

4. Stir all the fudge ingredients together in a mixing bowl until you have a thick mixture. Remove the flapjack mixture from the fridge, pour the fudge mixture on top, and return to the fridge for an hour or so to set. Alternatively, if you're impatient like me, put it in the freezer to set more quickly. Cut into 16 squares and store in an airtight container in the fridge for up to a week.

STICKY TOFFEE PUDDING

Sticky toffee pudding was my late grandpa's absolute favorite dessert. He had the biggest sweet tooth ever, as well as the biggest heart. He also had the most wicked sense of humor, and recently my dad decided to compile a list of all his best one-liners, with input from the extended family, so that we don't forget them.

In honor of the late, great Roy Friedman, I decided it was time to re-create this iconic dessert Mrs. H—style for my family. So I began experimenting in earnest and came up with these moist, rich, intense, treacly, sweet, and of course sticky beauties.

* MAKES 16 SQUARES

1 cup pitted Medjool dates
1¼ cups almond milk (see page 18)
1⅓ cups ground almonds
6 tablespoons cashew butter (see tip, page 22)
½ cup coconut sugar
¼ cup olive oil
½ teaspoon ground ginger
½ teaspoon ground cinnamon

FOR THE TOFFEE SAUCE
½ cup plus 2 tablespoons coconut sugar
¼ cup coconut milk
2 teaspoons pure vanilla extract

1. Preheat the oven to 375°F. Line a shallow 8-inch square baking pan with parchment paper, or use a disposable aluminum pan (see page 48).

2. Chop the dates into small chunks and pop them in a saucepan with the almond milk. Simmer over medium heat for about 5 minutes, then let cool.

3. Mix together the ground lamonds, cashew butter, sugar, olive oil, ginger, and cinnamon in a mixing bowl, then pour in the date mixture and stir well to combine.

4. Pour the mixture into the prepared pan and bake for about 30 minutes, or until the top is spongy but the middle is still gooey. Let cool while you make the sauce.

5. To make the sauce, combine all the sauce ingredients in a small saucepan and simmer, stirring, for 5 minutes, or until well combined and starting to thicken.

6. Drizzle the sauce over the pudding, cut into 16 squares, and enjoy right away! Store leftovers in an airtight container in the fridge for up to 5 days. Gently warm through before serving.

THE WORLD'S BEST BROWNIES

When I was running my farmers' market stall, my dad decided to tell every customer that, having tried all the other brownies, these were the best in the world. His sales strategy worked and they sold like hot cakes, so the name stuck. My stepmom adores them, too, so I often make them for her and my dad as a little thank-you when they babysit. No wonder they always offer!

Brownies can be a tricky thing to get right, especially if you are angling for the accolade of "world's best brownies," which I most certainly am. They need to be ever so slightly crisp on top, chewy on the outsides and soft and gooey in the middle. It's taken a lot of batches and a lot of taste-testing (shoutouts to my ever-willing guinea pigs), but one fateful Saturday morning I decided to try one more variation, and I nailed it! I'm so confident in their amazingness, I urge you to stop what you are doing, or as soon as you can, go buy the ingredients and make them. I promise, they will not disappoint. ✱ MAKES 16 BROWNIES

1 cup cacao powder
½ cup coconut oil
1 cup pitted Medjool dates
½ cup pure maple syrup
2 flaxseed "eggs" (see page 13)
½ cup ground almonds
½ cup cashew butter (see tip, page 22)
pinch of Himalayan pink salt
1 tablespoon water, or more if needed
½ cup walnuts

1. Preheat the oven to 300°F. Line a shallow 8-inch square baking pan with parchment paper, or use a disposable aluminum pan (see page 48).

2. Process all the ingredients except the walnuts in a food processor for a couple of minutes, or until a smooth and sticky mixture forms. If it's too sticky (i.e., if it forms a big ball), just add a little more water, a tablespoon at a time, until you get the desired consistency.

3. Crumble the walnuts into the brownie mixture and stir in, then spoon the mixture into the prepared pan and press down evenly with the back of the spoon.

4. Bake for 25 minutes, then let cool for 30 minutes (the brownies will continue to cook after they are taken out of the oven). When the waiting is finally over, cut into 16 squares and enjoy! Store in an airtight container at room temperature for up to 5 days or freeze for up to 2 months.

RAW FROSTED HAZELNUT-COCONUT BROWNIES

I'm extremely impatient. I've got better since having a child, as I think having your patience tested on a daily (sometimes hourly) basis makes you develop techniques to be more relaxed and calm in the face of challenging situations. Funny thing is that Baby H is super impatient, too, so no guessing where she got that from.

My impatience extends to my baking—waiting for items to bake in the oven feels like torture, and waiting for them to cool before I can frost them (and, let's face it, eat them) is even worse. Which is why I love raw brownies.

These are just heaven—all hazelnutty and chocolaty, and with the perfect amount of sweet, creamy coconut. ✳ MAKES 16 BROWNIES

2½ cups hazelnuts
⅔ cup desiccated coconut
1½ cups pitted Medjool dates
¼ cup coconut milk
½ cup cacao powder
pinch of Himalayan pink salt (optional)

FOR THE FROSTING
1 cup coconut milk
5 Medjool dates, pitted
¼ cup cacao powder
2 tablespoons coconut oil

1. Line a shallow 8-inch square baking pan with parchment paper, or use a disposable aluminum pan (see page 48).

2. Process the hazelnuts, desiccated coconut, dates, coconut milk, cacao powder, and salt in a food processor for 2 to 3 minutes, until a sticky mixture forms. Spoon the mixture into the prepared pan and press down evenly with the back of the spoon.

3. To make the frosting, process all the frosting ingredients in the food processor for about a minute, until creamy, stopping halfway through to scrape down the sides of the bowl if you need to.

4. Spoon the frosting evenly over the brownies. Cut into 16 squares and enjoy right away or place in the fridge for an hour or two to set a bit first. Store in an airtight container in the fridge for up to a week or freeze for up to 2 months.

CHOCOLATE-ORANGE FROSTED BLACK BEAN BROWNIES

Black beans and avocado—sounds like the perfect beginnings to a successful fajita night, doesn't it? But these ingredients are also a very useful combination when it comes to brownie making. I never tell my taste testers what's actually in my recipes before they try them because I like to know whether they can tell if there are any incognito fruits or veggies hiding out in my latest baked good. I can happily report that the black beans in these brownies and the avocado in this frosting safely smuggled themselves into my testers' tummies without anyone having the slightest notion.

The black beans give the brownies an amazingly moist and gooey texture in the middle. They are also slightly crisp on the outside, perfectly chocolaty with a hint of tangy orange (which they did taste) and just the right amount of sweetness—exactly how brownies should be! The avocado makes the frosting wonderfully creamy; it's literally the icing on the cake!

✳ MAKES 16 BROWNIES

✳ TOP TIP

To make these nut-free, simply replace the almond milk with oat or coconut milk (see page 18), and swap out the chopped pecans for cacao nibs.

FOR THE BROWNIES

3 tablespoons coconut oil, plus more for greasing
1 (14-ounce) can black beans, drained and rinsed
¾ cup pitted Medjool dates
½ cup gluten-free rolled oats
½ cup cacao powder
finely grated zest of 1 orange
2 tablespoons ground flaxseeds
¼ teaspoon Himalayan pink salt
½ cup almond milk (see page 18)
½ cup chopped pecans

FOR THE FROSTING

1 ripe avocado, halved and pitted
5 Medjool dates, pitted
5 tablespoons cacao powder
finely grated zest of ¼ orange
¼ cup coconut oil

1. To make the brownies, preheat the oven to 350°F. Grease a shallow 8-inch square baking pan, or use a disposable aluminum pan (see page 48).

2. Process all the brownie ingredients except the pecans in a food processor for about 2 minutes, or until smooth. Stir in the pecans, then spoon the mixture into the prepared pan. Gently press down evenly with the back of the spoon. Bake for 35 minutes—they may still seem quite gooey in the middle, but they will continue cooking as they cool. Let cool for 30 minutes.

3. To make the frosting, scoop the avocado flesh into the food processor, add the remaining frosting ingredients, and process for about a minute, or until smooth, stopping halfway through to scrape down the sides of the bowl if necessary.

4. Spoon the frosting evenly over the cooled brownies. Cut into 16 squares and enjoy right away or place in the fridge for an hour to set a bit first. Store in an airtight container in the fridge for up to 5 days or freeze for up to 2 months.

BLONDIES HAVE MORE YUM

You may be familiar with brownies, but have you heard of blondies? If not, I'm about to totally rock your world. This sweet treat uses vanilla and brown sugar in place of the cocoa in traditional brownies, hence the name.

Blondies are a massive hit in our household, and for good reason—they are sweet, fudgy, fruity, chocolaty, and just generally amazing. The optional addition of strawberries takes these to another level, as the flavors go together so well. Did I mention there is a secret ingredient here? Well, I guess the secret's out now, but this recipe uses chickpeas, although I promise you won't be able to taste them at all! Don't believe me? Try them for yourself! * MAKES 16 BLONDIES

½ cup gluten-free rolled oats
1 cup ground almonds
1 cup drained and rinsed canned chickpeas
1 cup cashew butter (see tip, page 22)
⅔ cup pure maple syrup
½ cup almond milk (see page 18)
2 tablespoons ground flaxseeds
3 tablespoons coconut oil, melted
⅔ cup hulled strawberries, plus extra whole strawberries for topping, if desired
½ cup raw chocolate (whatever variety you prefer, see page 31), chopped into small chunks plus more for drizzling, if desired

1. Preheat the oven to 350°F. Line a shallow 8-inch square baking pan with parchment paper, or use a disposable aluminum pan (see page 48).

2. Process the oats in a food processor or high-speed blender for about 30 seconds, until they form a flour. Add all the remaining ingredients except the strawberries and chocolate and process for a minute or so more, until smooth.

3. Pour the mixture into a mixing bowl and stir in the hulled strawberries and chocolate, then spoon it into the prepared pan and gently press down evenly with the back of the spoon.

4. Bake for 40 minutes, or until the blondies begin to look golden on top and a skewer inserted into the center comes out clean. Let cool.

5. If desired, melt ¼ cup chopped chocolate, drizzle it over the blondies, and let set. Cut the blondies into 16 squares and top with additional strawberries, if you wish. Store in an airtight container at room temperature for up to 5 days or freeze for up to 2 months.

*TOP TIP

When you drain the chickpeas, don't discard the water that they're soaked in. This liquid is called aquafaba, which is another plant-based ingredient that can be used in the place of egg whites. Save it to make The Quintessential Victoria Sponge (page 154) at a later date.

THE ROCKY ROAD TO DELICIOUSNESS

In college, as a self-confessed chocoholic with extremely limited baking skills, I used to adore making rocky road. By the time I graduated, I had perfected my art, and at every work bake-off I would whip up a batch of my signature dish, to the delight of my colleagues.

Although they tasted divine, they weren't doing any good for my insides (or my outsides, for that matter), so when I ditched the dairy and scrapped the sugar, those babies were the first to go. But luckily I've created a healthier version, which, in my opinion, tastes even better. They are so easy to make, and will leave your friends and colleagues wondering how such plant-based deliciousness could possibly exist.

✱ MAKES 16 SQUARES

FOR THE "COOKIE"
1 cup ground almonds
½ cup pitted Medjool dates

FOR THE CHOCOLATE
1 cup cacao butter or coconut oil
3 tablespoons cacao powder
3 tablespoons pure maple syrup
2 tablespoons almond butter

FOR THE FILLING
⅓ cup raisins, dried cranberries, or goji berries
⅓ cup whole cashews or macadamia nuts

1. Preheat the oven to 350°F. Line a baking sheet with parchment paper.

2. To make the "cookie," process the ground almonds and dates in a food processor until they form a sticky mixture. Spoon onto the lined baking sheet and press down evenly with the back of the spoon into a layer about ½ inch thick. Bake for 10 minutes, or until golden brown on top. Let cool.

3. Meanwhile, line a shallow 8-inch square baking pan with parchment paper, or use a disposable aluminum pan (see page 48). To make the chocolate, melt the cacao butter or coconut oil in a saucepan over low heat, then stir in the cacao powder, maple syrup, and almond butter. Remove from the heat and stir in the desired filling ingredients. Mash the "cookie" into chunks and stir it into the chocolate mixture.

4. Spoon the mixture into the prepared pan and place in the fridge for 2 to 3 hours to set. Cut into 16 squares and store in an airtight container in the fridge for up to a week or freeze for up to 2 months.

BLACKBERRY AND PEAR CRUMBLE

When I was younger, we would go on vacation to Cornwall and stuff our faces with blackberries that grew on the bushes along the coastal paths. My mom would bring containers and we would fill them up with blackberries, which she would use to make the most amazing of all crumbles. She usually combined the blackberries with apples, but sometimes she paired them with pears (see what I did there?), and those were my favorites. There is just something about juicy, sweet pears that works so well with the tartness of the berries.

So this recipe is a little throwback to one of my favorite, comforting desserts growing up, and hopefully it will become one of Baby H's favorites, too. My mom now lives down in Cornwall by the sea, so whenever we go down there in the summer, it's coastal walks with containers at the ready.

✳ SERVES 8

1 cup blackberries
4 pears, peeled, cored, and cut into chunks
2 tablespoons pure maple syrup
2½ cups gluten-free rolled oats
½ cup pecans
⅓ cup slivered almonds
pinch of Himalayan pink salt
7 tablespoons pure maple syrup
¼ cup coconut oil, melted
coconut yogurt or ice cream, for serving

1. Preheat the oven to 350°F.

2. Toss together the blackberries, pears, and maple syrup in a mixing bowl, then place them in a medium-sized baking dish and spread them out evenly over the bottom.

3. Process half the oats and all the pecans in a food processor for 10 seconds, then pour them into a separate mixing bowl. Add the remaining oats, the slivered almonds, and the salt and stir together, then mix in the maple syrup and melted coconut oil until you have a crumbly mixture.

4. Spoon the oat mixture evenly over the fruit, then bake for 30 minutes, or until golden on top. Serve hot from the oven with coconut yogurt or ice cream.

CHERRY BAKEWELL SLICES

When I was little and had friends round for tea, we would have sandwiches in triangles (because I insisted they tasted better than squares), sliced fruit and a selection of a certain man's "exceedingly good" cakes. The fondant fancies never took my fancy and the Battenberg cake didn't float my boat, but I was always partial to a cherry bakewell.

For anyone who doesn't know, the traditional bakewell tart has a pastry base, with layers of jelly and frangipane topped with slivered almonds. Some versions have a layer of icing on top, but I think I prefer the original. The cherry and almond flavors go so well together, and it really is a treat to eat—or dare I say, exceedingly better! ✳ MAKES 16 SLICES

FOR THE BASE LAYER
2 cups ground almonds
⅓ cup buckwheat flour
pinch of Himalayan pink salt
5 tablespoons pure maple syrup
¼ cup almond butter
2 tablespoons coconut oil, melted

FOR THE CHERRY FILLING
2 cups frozen pitted cherries
2 tablespoons pure maple syrup

FOR THE FRANGIPANE
1 cup ground almonds
2 tablespoons pure maple syrup
2 tablespoons almond butter
1 tablespoon coconut oil, melted
½ cup slivered almonds

1. Preheat the oven to 350°F. Line a shallow 8-inch square baking pan with parchment paper, or use a disposable aluminum pan (see page 48).

2. To make the base layer, mix together the ground almonds, buckwheat flour, and salt in a mixing bowl, then stir in the wet ingredients to form a sticky dough.

3. Spoon the mixture into the prepared pan and press down evenly with the back of the spoon.

4. To make the cherry filling, blend the cherries and maple syrup in a blender for about 30 seconds so that the fruit is still a little bit chunky. Pour the filling over the base layer and spread it out evenly.

5. To make the frangipane, mix together all the frangipane ingredients except the slivered almonds in a mixing bowl. Distribute teaspoons of the frangipane over the top of the cherry layer, then gently spread it evenly across the cherry layer without disrupting it too much. Sprinkle the slivered almonds evenly over the top. Bake for 20 minutes. Let cool.

6. Cut into 16 slices. Store in an airtight container in the fridge for up to a week or freeze for up to 2 months.

I knew when I was writing this book that I had to dedicate a chapter to my love of cookies. To misquote Elizabeth Barrett Browning: "How do I love cookie? Let me count the ways." And count the ways I shall:

1. Nothing, and I mean nothing, goes better with a cup of tea than a good old cookie. Whether you savor it or scarf it, dip it or dunk it, there is no denying that it makes the perfect teatime snack.

2. Cookie offer a taste of nostalgia—visits to friends' houses, picnics in the park, those mixed-cookie boxes where everyone wanted (and fought over) the same ones, and post-swimming pick-me-ups; a childhood sprinkled with cookie crumbs.

3. Cookies are also ridiculously easy to make. Most of these recipes require just a few ingredients, a mixing bowl, and the oven. Which leads me to . . .

4. Baking time. This lot doesn't take very long to cook. The sooner they bake, the sooner we eat, so this is (quite literally) a good thing in my book.

I could go on and on, but I'm a smart cookie when it comes to giving the people what they want. Let's do this.

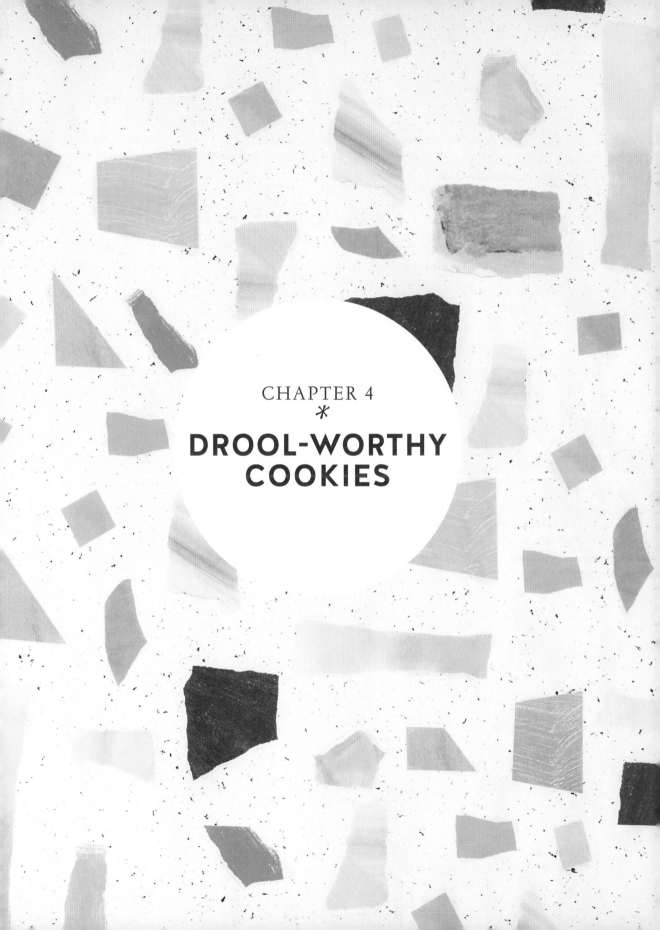

CHAPTER 4

*

DROOL-WORTHY COOKIES

CHOCOLATE "HOBNOB" COOKIES

There are some recipes that I like to call my "homeland," the very essence of what I stand for—simple, easy, delicious, and often chocolaty. These cookies are a prime example, and one of the most popular recipes from my blog.

When I was a child, my brother and I used to have the loveliest Czech babysitter. As all little people do, we loved convincing adults to teach us swear words in different languages so we could use them in the school playground or wherever without getting told off, so anyone who spoke a foreign language was a valuable resource to us. Our babysitter didn't mind indulging us in our favorite pastime (anything to keep us occupied while our parents were out), so she taught us a couple of words. One such word was *hovno*, apparently Czech for "shit," but it sounded like "hobnob" to us, which we thought was hilarious, and of course it stuck.

These aren't *hovno* in the slightest. In fact, if you took them to a celebrity party, they would have you "hobnobbing" with the rich and famous in no time.

✻ MAKES ABOUT 12 COOKIES

FOR THE COOKIES
1¼ cups gluten-free rolled oats
¾ cup ground almonds
½ cup cashew butter (see tip, page 22), or any other nut or seed butter
½ cup pure maple syrup
½ teaspoon Himalayan pink salt

FOR THE CHOCOLATE TOPPING
½ cup cacao butter
3 tablespoons pure maple syrup
3 tablespoons cacao powder
1 tablespoon cashew butter (see tip, page 22)

1. Preheat the oven to 350°F. Line a baking sheet with parchment paper.

2. To make the cookies, combine the ingredients in a mixing bowl and knead together until everything is well combined and the mixture comes together into a dough.

3. Divide the dough into 12 pieces, roll into balls, and flatten them into discs about ½ inch thick. Place on the lined baking sheet and bake for 15 minutes, or until lightly golden, then let cool completely.

4. To make the chocolate topping, melt the cacao butter in a heatproof bowl over a saucepan half full of gently boiling water over medium heat, then stir in the other ingredients.

5. Dip the cookies in the chocolate mixture (you might want to do this a couple of times for each cookies) and then drizzle any extra chocolate on top. Put them in the fridge for a couple of minutes so that the chocolate sets before eating. Store in an airtight container in the fridge for up to 3 days or freeze for 1 month.

GINGERBREAD PEOPLE

I don't like gender stereotyping, which is, I have come to realize, embedded deep in our society. If someone says the word "midwife" or "florist" or "ballet dancer," most of us would think of a woman, whereas if they said "stockbroker" or "construction worker" and "truck driver," men would probably come to mind. In this book you won't find any such assumptions. Yes, I may be a housewife who bakes, but let's skirt around that issue—pun intended, of course. Unless you are adding genitalia to your gingerbread men (in which case I would like to know where you got your cookie cutters from), then why do they have to be men? Why not women, children, or anything in between?

✳ MAKES 6 TO 8 GINGERBREAD PEOPLE

1 cup ground almonds
1 cup buckwheat flour, plus extra for dusting
2 tablespoons ground ginger
6 tablespoons pure maple syrup
2 flaxseed "eggs" (see page 13)
1 tablespoon coconut oil, melted

1. Preheat the oven to 350°F. Line a baking sheet with parchment paper.

2. Mix together the ground almonds, buckwheat flour, and ginger in a mixing bowl, then stir in the maple syrup, flaxseed "eggs," and melted coconut oil and knead into a sticky dough.

3. Transfer the dough to a work surface dusted with a little buckwheat flour. Roll out the dough with a rolling pin until it's about ¼ inch thick, then use a gingerbread cookie cutter to cut out your people. Gather together the trimmings, reroll the dough, and cut out more cookies until you've used all the dough.

4. Place the cookies on the lined baking sheet and bake for about 15 minutes, or until they are a little golden on top. Let them cool before eating or decorating. Store in an airtight container at room temperature for up to 5 days or freeze for 1 month.

✳ TOP TIP
Decorate using some melted raw chocolate (see page 31) to draw features and clothes, and use it to stick on berries, nuts, or cacao nibs.

BOURBON COOKIES

Did you know that Bourbons have been around since 1910? That's only a few years after the end of Queen Victoria's epic reign, although rumor has it she was more of a sponge cake kinda gal. But Bourbons have their own royal heritage: they are named after the House of Bourbon, a family who were big names in Europe since the sixteenth century, and who clearly loved a good cookie. Upon further research, I discovered this isn't true, but I prefer it to the real story—it's named after two places, Bourneville and Bonn—so let's stick with it. I also found out that the Bourbon was the first cookie consumed on the moon, by Buzz Aldrin. He may not have been the first man to walk on the moon, but surely this is a better accolade. One small snack for man, one giant leap for mankind. One final little gem before we get into the recipe: the reason Bourbons have holes in them is to let the steam out so they don't crack or break. ✳ MAKES ABOUT 14 SANDWICH COOKIES

FOR THE COOKIES
⅓ cup gluten-free rolled oats
½ cup buckwheat flour, plus extra for dusting
10 tablespoons cacao powder
½ cup pure maple syrup
6 tablespoons coconut oil
pinch of Himalayan pink salt

FOR THE FILLING
¼ cup cacao powder
3 tablespoons pure maple syrup
2 tablespoons tahini
1 tablespoon coconut milk

1. Preheat the oven to 350°F. Line a baking sheet with parchment paper.

2. To make the cookies, process all the cookie ingredients in a food processor or blender for about 4 minutes, or until you have a sticky dough.

3. Transfer the dough to a work surface dusted with a little buckwheat flour. Roll out the dough with a rolling pin until it's about ¼ inch thick, then use the lid of a small tin of mints to cut out rectangular shapes (I use a silicone bar mold), or whatever shaped cutter you have to hand. Gather together the trimmings, reroll the dough, and cut out more cookies until you've used all the dough.

4. Place the cookies on the lined baking sheet, prick them with a fork (can't be forgetting those holes!), and bake for 15 minutes. Let the cookies cool completely while you make the filling.

5. Mix together all the filling ingredients in a mixing bowl until you have a thick, chocolaty mixture. Spoon the filling onto the flat side of half the biscuits and sandwich with the remaining cookies. Store the cookies in an airtight container in the fridge for up to 3 days or freeze for 1 month.

PEANUT BUTTER CHOCOLATE CHUNK COOKIES

When you think of the word "cookie," what do you think of? My guess is the kind of cookie that the Cookie Monster eats—you know, the one that looks like the cookie emoji, golden in color with chocolate chips. Am I right? Well, my friends, these are those cookies. We are talking dark golden chewy yet crunchy cookies, studded with delicious raw chocolaty chunks; nutty and sweet, with just the right hint of salt. These are the kind of cookies that glasses of milk were made to accompany, the ones you'll want to make over and over again, and then some. Just be warned: they have a tendency to turn regular, rational, normal people into full-blown cookie monsters, so be sure you've made enough to go around! ✳ MAKES ABOUT 6 TO 8 COOKIES

1 cup peanut flour (see tip)
½ cup peanut butter (see page 21)
8 Medjool dates, pitted
2 tablespoons coconut oil
1 ripe banana, peeled
2 tablespoons water
pinch of Himalayan pink salt, or more to taste
½ cup chopped raw chocolate (whatever variety you prefer; see page 31)

1. Preheat the oven to 350°F. Line a baking sheet with parchment paper.

2. Process all the ingredients except the chocolate in a food processor for about 30 seconds, or until you have a sticky dough, then stir in the chocolate chunks.

3. Divide the dough into 6 to 8 pieces, roll into balls, and flatten them into discs about ½ inch thick.

4. Place on the lined baking sheet and bake for about 15 minutes, or until a dark golden on top, then let cool before digging in. Store in an airtight container at room temperature for up to 5 days or freeze for 1 month.

✳ TOP TIP

If you don't have peanut flour on hand, you can substitute ground almonds. Or roast 1 cup raw blanched peanuts (see page 21), let cool, then process in a food processor or high-speed blender for about 20 seconds until they form a flour.

SANDWICH COOKIES

Despite always being a total chocolate fiend, my favorite cookies used to be jelly sandwich cookies. My brother and I would have in-depth, philosophical discussions about the best way to eat them. Should you nibble around the edge and leave the middle until the end? Or is it better to prise off the top layer and eat the non-jelly-covered side as an amuse-bouche, before enjoying the finest of open-face cookie sandwiches? I've even eaten one upside down to see if it would taste better, which actually just gave me the hiccups.

What I do know is that these cookies are better than the originals. The almond flavor in the cookies works beautifully to balance out the tart fruity flavors of the jelly, and every bite is delightful. However you eat them. ✱ MAKES 4 OR 5 SANDWICH COOKIES

⅔ cup ground almonds
½ cup buckwheat flour, plus extra for dusting
pinch of Himalayan pink salt
3 tablespoons pure maple syrup
2 tablespoons coconut oil,
    softened but not melted (see tip)
½ teaspoon pure vanilla extract
Berry Chia Jelly (page 26), for filling

1. Preheat the oven to 350°F. Line a baking sheet with parchment paper.

2. Mix together the ground almonds, buckwheat flour, and salt in a mixing bowl, then add the maple syrup, coconut oil, and vanilla and knead together until you have a dough.

3. Transfer the dough to a work surface dusted with a little buckwheat flour. Roll out the dough with a rolling pin until it's about ¼ inch thick, then use a round cutter to cut out 8 or 10 cookies. I have a cutter with a heart shape in the center all ready to stamp out, but if you don't have one of these, use something like a bottle top to cut out a little circle from the center of half the cookies for the tops of the cookie sandwiches.

4. Place the cookies on the lined baking sheet and bake for 15 minutes, then let them cool completely.

5. Place a teaspoon of the jelly on each whole cookie and sandwich with the cookies with cut-out centers. Store in an airtight container in the fridge for up to 3 days or freeze for 1 month.

✱TOP TIP

You want the coconut oil to be soft enough so that you can cream it into the dough (as you would do with butter), but not too soft, otherwise the mixture won't be as easy to cut into shapes. So if it's super hard, put it in an ovenproof dish and pop it in the oven for 30 seconds while the oven is preheating, to help it soften.

MAPLE-PECAN CRUNCH COOKIES

My daughter has definitely inherited her mother's chatterbox nature, as well as her father's sweet tooth—OK, her mother's sweet tooth, too. I try not to give her too many sweet things, but sometimes when the oven is on, cookies are a-baking, and the house is filled with a rich, sweet aroma, I hear the pitter-patter of little feet, followed by a little voice saying, "Mooooore." She doesn't know yet that to have "more" you need to have had "some," but I hope this means two things: 1) the smell of baking cookies will always transport her back to carefree childhood times; and 2) she will always ask for "more" and never be afraid to go after what she wants, even if right now what she wants are cookies that are too hot to be eaten. ✳ MAKES 12 COOKIES

1½ cups gluten-free rolled oats
½ cup buckwheat flour
½ cup roughly chopped pecans
½ teaspoon ground cinnamon
pinch of Himalayan pink salt
¼ cup coconut oil, melted
½ cup pure maple syrup

1. Preheat the oven to 350°F. Line a baking sheet with parchment paper.

2. Mix together the oats, buckwheat flour, pecans, cinnamon, and salt in a mixing bowl, then add the melted coconut oil and maple syrup and stir until you have a sticky dough.

3. Divide the dough into 12 pieces, roll into balls, and flatten them into little discs, then place them on the lined baking sheet.

4. Bake the cookies for about 10 minutes, or until a little golden on top. Let cool and then tuck in! Store in an airtight container at room temperature for up to 5 days or freeze for 1 month.

SALTED ALMOND BUTTER CARAMEL VIENNESE WHIRLS

Viennese whirls are definitely the best food to have come out of Vienna. Although apparently they are about as Austrian as a hot dog, but they were supposedly "inspired" by Austrian cookies. Cool. I used to love these when I was younger because I adored shortbread, but I would also pick these when I had to choose just one cookie, as it actually meant I got two for one, thus totally beating the system and winning at life.

Even though these days I can have double cookies whenever I want, there is still something a little special about these. The traditional version combines a shortbread cookie with a cream-and-jelly filling, but as you might have noticed, this ain't no traditional cookbook, so I've gone a little maverick on you guys.

✱ MAKES 4 SANDWICH COOKIES

FOR THE COOKIES

1 cup ground almonds
½ cup almond butter
¼ cup pure maple syrup
2 tablespoons coconut oil, softened but not melted (see tip, page 74)
1 tablespoon maca powder (optional, for a more malty flavor)
½ teaspoon pure vanilla extract
pinch of Himalayan pink salt

FOR THE FILLING

¼ cup chilled full-fat coconut milk (see page 12)
½ batch Sticky Salted Date Caramel (page 28)

1. Preheat the oven to 325°F. Line a baking sheet with parchment paper.

2. To make the cookies, combine all the cookie ingredients to a large mixing bowl and beat together until the mixture is light and gooey.

3. Transfer the mixture to a piping bag fitted with a large closed star tip. Pipe the mixture onto the lined baking sheet in a small circle, as if you were drawing a spiral, starting from the outside and working your way inward to the center. Repeat to pipe another seven small circles.

4. Bake the cookies for 12 minutes, or until golden, then let them cool completely.

5. To fill the cookies, spoon the coconut milk onto half the cookies and the salted caramel onto the remainder, then sandwich them together. Store in an airtight container in the fridge for up to 3 days or freeze for 1 month.

CHOCOLATE-COVERED "OREO" COOKIES

Oreos have a lot to answer for. On one particular trip to the US some years ago, I got so excited at all the weird and wonderful new flavors that weren't available in the UK that I bought multiple packs of each. Cue my baggage being overweight and costing more than I bargained for on the way home. Land of the free? I think not. It turned out that the best ones in my haul were those covered in chocolate. Who would have thought a chocolate biscuit could be made even more delicious by covering it in chocolate?

These days my suitcase is overweight for other reasons—namely copious amounts of toys and snacks. But my love for Oreos (especially chocolate-covered ones) remains, so I wanted to share my take on them with you. No plane ticket needed.

✱ MAKES 6 SANDWICH COOKIES

1¼ cups cacao powder
1 cup ground almonds
½ cup buckwheat flour
6 tablespoons pure maple syrup
5 tablespoons coconut oil, melted
5 tablespoons cashew butter (see tip, page 22)

FOR THE FILLING
¼ cup raw cashews,
   soaked in water for at least 4 hours, then drained
¼ cup coconut milk
2 tablespoons coconut oil
¼ teaspoon pure vanilla extract
2 tablespoons pure maple syrup

½ batch Raw Milk Chocolate
   (page 31), melted, for coating

1. Preheat the oven to 350°F. Line a baking sheet with parchment paper.

2. Mix together the cacao powder, ground almonds, and buckwheat flour in a mixing bowl, then stir in the maple syrup, melted coconut oil, and cashew butter and knead until you have a smooth dough.

3. Divide the dough into 12 pieces, roll into balls, and flatten them into discs about ½ inch thick. Place the cookies on the lined baking sheet and bake for 10 minutes, then let cool completely.

4. Meanwhile, to make the filling, process all the filling ingredients in a food processor until they form a smooth, creamy mixture. It may seem quite liquid, but don't worry–place it in the fridge for about 30 minutes and it will set (by which time the cookies will have cooled).

5. Spoon the filling onto half the cookies and squish down the other halves on top to make six delicious sandwiches. Place in the freezer for an hour.

6. Remove the cookies from the freezer and coat them, one by one, in the melted chocolate; give them a couple of coats for good measure. Place the cookies in the fridge for 10 minutes to set the chocolate. Store in an airtight container in the fridge for up to 5 days or freeze for 1 month.

CINNAMON, OAT AND RAISIN COOKIES

I'm trying to do my bit to reduce waste and recycle more, since, as the saying goes, we inherit the earth from our ancestors but we need to look after it for our children. But saving the earth doesn't need to cost the earth. Not only is making your own nut milks cheaper (and they're nicer tasting, too, in my opinion), it saves on plastic packaging and, as a bonus, you get a valuable by-product, the nut pulp, which is absolutely fantastic for baking. So here is a "recyclpe" (that's a recycling recipe) that will knock your socks off . . .

✳ MAKES 6 TO 8 SMALL COOKIES

½ cup pulp from making Classic Almond Milk (page 18), or ⅓ cup ground almonds plus ¼ cup almond milk
1 cup gluten-free rolled oats
3 tablespoons golden raisins
2 tablespoons coconut oil
3 tablespoons pure maple syrup
1 teaspoon ground cinnamon

1. Preheat the oven to 350°F. Line a baking sheet with parchment paper.

2. Give the almond milk pulp a little squeeze to get rid of some of the excess liquid, but don't worry about doing it too much, as it shouldn't be too dry either. Pop the pulp into a mixing bowl with the oats and raisins and give it all a big stir.

3. Melt the coconut oil in a small saucepan, then stir in the maple syrup and cinnamon. Pour the mixture over the oat mixture and stir well so that you end up with a dough.

4. Divide the dough into 6 to 8 pieces, roll into balls, and flatten them into discs about ½ inch thick, or use cookie cutters if you're going for the fancy look!

5. Place the cookies on the lined baking sheet and bake for 15 to 20 minutes, until they are golden on top. Let cool completely. Store in an airtight container at room temperature for up to 5 days or freeze for 1 month.

TRIPLE CHOCOLATE DOUGHNUTS

In December 2017, when Baby H was almost eighteen months old, I thought I might make us some doughnuts to celebrate Hanukkah, the Jewish festival of light. Let's just say that with her and Mr. H around, these bad boys did not last anywhere near the full eight days. If they had, I think that would have been the real miracle of Hanukkah.

These doughnuts are soft and fluffy with a little bit of gooeyness, studded with chocolate, and covered in heavenly chocolate glaze. How long will they last in your household, I wonder?

✳ MAKES 8 DOUGHNUTS

FOR THE DOUGHNUTS
½ cup ground almonds
½ cup buckwheat flour
½ cup cacao powder
½ cup pure maple syrup
¼ cup coconut oil, melted
¼ cup unsweetened applesauce (or puree ½ apple)
pinch of Himalayan pink salt
¾ cup almond milk (see page 18)
¼ cup small chunks raw chocolate (whatever variety you prefer; see page 31), (optional)

FOR THE GLAZE
6 tablespoons cacao powder
6 tablespoons pure maple syrup
2 tablespoons coconut oil, melted

1. Preheat the oven to 350°F. Grease 8 wells of a doughnut pan (or use a silicone doughnut mold).

2. To make the doughnuts, process all the doughnut ingredients except the chocolate in a food processor until you have a lovely sticky mixture. (If you don't have a food processor, mix together the ground almonds, buckwheat flour, and cacao powder in a mixing bowl, then mix in the maple syrup, coconut oil, applesauce, salt, and almond milk.) Stir in the chocolate (if using), then divide the mixture among the prepared wells of the pan.

3. Bake for 15 to 20 minutes, until a skewer inserted into the center comes out clean. Let cool while you make the glaze.

4. To make the glaze, combine all the glaze ingredients in a mixing bowl and stir until you have the most decadent and rich chocolate.

5. Dunk the tops of the cooled doughnuts, one by one, into the glaze and get ready for a taste sensation! Store in an airtight container for up to a week in the fridge or freeze for 1 month.

I've loved cheesecake for a very long time now, and I think it's because of the texture: a deliciously melt-in-your-mouth, creamy topping balanced by a crunchy biscuit base. Cheesecake is to desserts what Kate Moss or Cara Delevingne are to the fashion world; it's so incredibly versatile, it works with any flavor, and you can easily make it look catwalk-ready with just a few decorative touches.

I'm totally aware of the huge, cheese-shaped elephant in the room here, but this chapter is testament to the fact that you don't need cheese to make the most indulgent and moreish "cheesecakes" under the sun. It really is simple to create the most amazing plant-based versions from just a few natural ingredients. I've got so many favorite flavor combinations and variations that it was very hard to decide which ones to include in this book. I'm sure of one thing, though—there is definitely a "cheesecake" (or nine) in here for you, whether you're a peanut butter nutter, loco for cocoa, a fruit fiend, or even nut-free.

CHAPTER 5

*

NO-CHEESE RAW "CHEESECAKES" & SLICES

QUADRUPLE CHOCOLATE "CHEESECAKE"

Much like the fashion world, every couple of months I decide that particular things are "out" and others are now very much "in," and that includes the foods I eat. There are, however, some things that I never tire of, those that are just "me" through and through. Chocolate is a prime example. It is to my life what a classic Chanel handbag is to any chic fashionista: classic, timeless, and incredibly versatile.

Unlike fashion though, when it comes to chocolate, more is definitely more. You might have heard of double chocolate, and maybe even triple chocolate, but have you ever had quadruple chocolate? This dessert has a chocolaty base topped with swirls of white, milk, and dark chocolate "cheesecake," studded with raw chocolate chunks and drizzle. It's so divine and, like a classic handbag, will never go out of style.

✳ SERVES 10

FOR THE BASE LAYER
1 cup desiccated coconut
1 cup ground almonds
1 cup pitted Medjool dates
½ cup cacao powder
¼ cup water, plus more if needed

FOR THE CHOCOLATE LAYERS
1½ cups raw cashews,
    soaked in water for 4 hours, then drained
¾ cup cacao butter, melted
½ cup pure maple syrup
¼ cup coconut milk
pinch of Himalayan pink salt
½ cup cacao powder

¾ cup small chunks Raw Dark Chocolate
(page 31)

1. To make the base layer, process all the ingredients in a food processor for 2 to 3 minutes, until the mixture sticks together when you pinch it and there are no large chunks of dates left. If your dates aren't super soft, you may need to add a little extra water, a tablespoon at a time, but make sure the mixture doesn't get too wet. Spoon the mixture into an 8-inch springform pan and press down evenly with the back of the spoon. Place in the freezer while you make the chocolate layers.

2. To make the chocolate layers, have three medium mixing bowls ready. Process the cashews, ½ cup of the melted cacao butter, the maple syrup, coconut milk, and salt in the food processor for about 3 minutes, or until it forms a smooth, creamy liquid, stopping every minute or so to scrape down the sides of the bowl. Place one-third of the mixture in one of your bowls and set aside; this will be the white chocolate filling.

3. Add ¼ cup of the cacao powder to the mixture remaining in the food processor and process for 20 seconds. Set half of this mixture aside in another medium bowl; this will be the milk chocolate filling. Add the remaining ¼ cup cacao powder and the melted cacao butter to the food processor and process for 20 seconds, then pour the mixture into your third bowl; this will be the dark chocolate filling.

4. Remove the base layer from the freezer. Using three spoons, dollop large spoonfuls of the three chocolate mixtures, one by one, onto the base layer, sprinkling ½ cup of the chocolate chunks in as you go, then use a skewer to swirl them all together (but don't mix so much that you can't see the distinct shades of chocolate). Place in the freezer for 2 hours to set.

5. Melt the remaining ¼ cup raw chocolate in a heatproof bowl over a saucepan half-full of gently boiling water over medium heat. Remove the "cheesecake" from the pan and drizzle the melted chocolate on top. Serve or store in a freezerproof container in the freezer for up to 2 months; remove an hour before serving.

NEAPOLITAN "CHEESECAKE'

I'm very indecisive. Or am I? I just can't decide. Jokes aside, I've always found it incredibly hard to make even the smallest of choices. I think it stems from a fear of missing out, and it's especially bad in restaurants. When I was a child, we only really had a dessert when my grandparents came for dinner on a Friday, so it made my decision even more important. Luckily, when my mum bought Neapolitan ice cream, my dilemma was solved; I could have a little of all three in one go without needing to choose between them.

If, like me, you find that choosing desserts makes you stressed (is it a coincidence that "stressed" is "desserts" backward?) and you want a bit of the classic vanilla, some fruity strawberry, and a little rich chocolate all in one bite, then this is the dessert for you.

✳ SERVES 10

FOR THE BASE LAYER
2 cups pitted Medjool dates
1½ cups raw cashews
¼ cup cacao powder

FOR THE STRAWBERRY LAYER
2 ripe bananas, peeled
1 cup hulled strawberries, plus extra whole
  strawberries for garnish
1 cup raw cashews,
  soaked in water for at least 4 hours, then drained
2 tablespoons pure maple syrup
2 tablespoons coconut oil, melted

FOR THE VANILLA LAYER
1 cup raw cashews,
  soaked in water for at least 4 hours, then drained
1 cup chilled full-fat coconut milk (see page 12)
⅓ cup pure maple syrup
2 tablespoons coconut oil, melted
1 tablespoon pure vanilla extract

FOR THE CHOCOLATE LAYER
1 ripe avocado, halved, pitted, and peeled
1 ripe banana, peeled
⅓ cup pitted Medjool dates
⅓ cup cacao powder
2 tablespoons coconut oil, melted

1. To make the base layer, process all the ingredients in a food processor for a couple of minutes, or until a sticky mixture forms. Spoon the mixture into an 8-inch springform pan and press down evenly with the back of the spoon.

2. To make the strawberry layer, process all the ingredients in the food processor for a minute or so until creamy and smooth. Spoon the mixture on top of the base layer and spread it evenly. Place the "cheesecake" in the freezer for 15 minutes to set the strawberry layer.

3. Repeat step 2 with the ingredients for the vanilla layer, then the chocolate layer, placing the cheeseacke in the freezer to set each layer before adding the next. Garnish with strawberries just before serving. Store in a freezerproof container in the freezer for up to 2 months; remove an hour before serving.

WHITE CHOCOLATE AND RASPBERRY "CHEESECAKE"

At every Hollingsworth family gathering at my mother-in-law's, be it a Sunday roast or a birthday celebration, you can count on two things: first, that you will go home ridiculously full, and second, that a white chocolate and raspberry cheesecake will feature as part of the dessert buffet—for good reason. There is something undeniably perfect about the combination of tart, juicy raspberries with the rich, creamy sweetness of white chocolate.

It was only a matter of time, therefore, until I tried my hand at my own version, which is sweet, creamy, and chocolaty with just the right amount of fruitiness. Now when it's our turn to host a family gathering, this is what I make instead, and it seems to go down just as well! ✳ SERVES 10

FOR THE BASE LAYER
1½ cups desiccated coconut
1 cup raw cashews
1 cup pitted Medjool dates
½ teaspoon pure vanilla extract

FOR THE RASPBERRY AND WHITE CHOCOLATE FILLING
1½ cups raw cashews, soaked in water
   for at least 4 hours, then drained
⅔ cup coconut milk
½ cup pure maple syrup
¼ cup coconut oil, melted
½ teaspoon pure vanilla extract
1 cup cacao butter
1 cup raspberries, plus extra for garnish

FOR THE WHITE CHOCOLATE DRIZZLE (OPTIONAL)
¼ cup cacao butter
3 tablespoons coconut oil
2 tablespoons pure maple syrup
¼ teaspoon pure vanilla extract

1. To make the base layer, process all the ingredients in a food processor for a couple of minutes, until a sticky mixture forms. Spoon into an 8-inch springform pan and press down with the back of the spoon. Place in the freezer while you make the filling.

2. To make the filling, process the cashews, coconut milk, and maple syrup in the food processor or a high-speed blender for a couple of minutes, or until smooth and creamy. Pour into a bowl and stir in the melted coconut oil and vanilla. Add the cacao butter and mix in well. Finally, stir in the raspberries.

3. Spoon the "cheesecake" filling over the base layer. Return to the freezer for at least 2 hours to set.

4. If you're making the drizzle, melt the cacao butter and coconut oil in a heatproof bowl over a saucepan, half-full of gently boiling water over medium heat. Remove from the heat, add the maple syrup and vanilla, and stir until you have a smooth, glossy mixture. Just before serving, remove the "cheesecake" from the pan, drizzle with the white chocolate, and sprinkle with raspberries. Store leftovers in a freezerproof container in the freezer for up to 2 months; remove 1 to 2 hours before serving.

IMMUNE-BOOSTING LEMON-GINGER "CHEESECAKE" BITES

When I get a bit run-down or if I catch a cold, I will always make myself a little lemon-and-ginger concoction. The tartness of the lemon and the spiciness of the ginger are a great combination taste-wise, as well as having lots of amazing healing powers between them.

The last time I felt a bit poorly, I sat on the sofa snuggled up and sipping away and decided I needed to create a recipe showcasing these fabulous flavors, these bites being the result. The base layer tastes just like gingerbread, while the creamy "cheesecake" layer is refreshingly zingy at the same time as being gorgeously sweet thanks to the lemon and maple syrup, respectively.

✳ SERVES 16

FOR THE BASE LAYER
1¼ cups gluten-free rolled oats
1¼ cups raw cashews
1 cup pitted Medjool dates
1 thumb-sized piece fresh ginger, peeled
1 tablespoon coconut oil

FOR THE "CHEESECAKE" LAYER
1 cup raw cashews,
    soaked in water for at least 4 hours, then drained
1 cup coconut milk
½ cup coconut oil
½ teaspoon pure vanilla extract
¼ cup pure maple syrup
finely grated zest of 1 lemon

1. To make the base layer, process all the ingredients in a food processor for a couple of minutes, or until they form a big, sticky ball. Spoon the mixture into an 8-inch springform pan (I like to use a square one for this, for no reason in particular) and press down evenly with the back of the spoon.

2. To make the cheesecake layer, process all the ingredients for the "cheesecake" in the food processor or a high-speed blender until completely creamy, testing the mixture every minute or so. It should take about 5 minutes, but this will depend on the speed and power of your equipment.

3. Spoon the "cheesecake" mixture evenly on top of the base layer, then place in the freezer for at least 2 hours to set. Cut into 16 squares and serve or store in a freezerproof container in the freezer for up to 2 months; remove 1 hour before serving.

TIRAMISU "CHEESECAKE" SLICES

Until getting up early and being fully functional became a mandatory weekday activity, i.e., when I started work after college, I hadn't felt the need to try coffee, but when I realized it could help me feel less like a zombie, I was all over it like a rash. Having since changed my diet, lifestyle, and career, I now don't need a caffeine boost to wake me up in the mornings, but still adore the taste of coffee, and I love experimenting with it in desserts. This tiramisu (which means "pick me up" in Italian) "cheesecake" combines a coffee-and-walnut base layer with a chocolate-coffee mousse middle, finished with a vanilla cream layer on top. It's the perfect dessert for all my fellow coffee lovers out there. ✷ SERVES 10

FOR THE BASE LAYER
1 cup walnuts
1 cup pitted Medjool dates
1 teaspoon instant coffee granules
2 tablespoons cacao butter, melted
pinch of Himalayan pink salt
1 tablespoon water, or more if needed

FOR THE CHOCOLATE-COFFEE LAYER
1⅓ cups raw cashews,
    soaked in water for 4 hours, then drained
1¼ cups pitted Medjool dates
⅓ cup coconut milk
¼ cup cacao powder, plus extra for dusting
¼ cup cacao butter, melted
1 tablespoon coffee granules

FOR THE VANILLA CREAM LAYER
½ cup raw cashews,
    soaked in water for 4 hours, then drained
¼ cup coconut milk
2 tablespoons cacao butter, melted
2 tablespoons pure maple syrup
½ teaspoon pure vanilla extract

1. To make the base layer, process all the ingredients in a food processor until they form a sticky mixture. Spoon the mixture into an 8-inch springform pan and press down evenly with the back of the spoon. Place in the freezer while you make the chocolate coffee layer.

2. To make the coffee layer, process all the ingredients in the food processor for 2 to 3 minutes, until they form a smooth, chocolaty mixture. Remove the base layer from the freezer and spoon the chocolate-coffee mixture evenly on top. Return to the freezer while you make the vanilla cream layer.

3. To make the vanilla cream layer, process all the ingredients in the food processor until smooth, then spoon the vanilla mixture on top of the coffee layer and place in the fridge for 4 hours to set.

4. Dust the "cheesecake" with cacao powder, cut into slices, and serve. Store any leftovers in a freezerproof container in the freezer for up to 2 months; remove 1 to 2 hours before serving.

BLUEBERRY "CHEESECAKE" SLICES

Fruity, creamy, tart, sweet, and totally indulgent, these slices have got to be one of my favorite summer desserts. Baby H, a seasoned blueberry devotee, is also a big fan, although unfortunately for me, she does tend to make rather a lot of mess when she eats them. In fact, I could call these "blueberry striptease-cake slices," as one by one all my items of clothing will get sticky little blueberry handprints on them, and one by one, I'll have to take them off, put them in the wash, and then lay them out in the sun to avoid stains. Luckily, in the summer we can just hang out in our swimmies by the baby pool, so that's partly why I tend to make these more then. But they are delicious all year round; just make sure you're wearing dark-colored clothes if you're giving them to little people!

✳ SERVES 16

FOR THE BASE LAYER
1 cup whole almonds
1½ cups pitted Medjool dates
2 tablespoons coconut oil

FOR THE BLUEBERRY LAYER
2 cups raw cashews,
    soaked in water for 4 hours, then drained
6 tablespoons pure maple syrup
1 cup frozen blueberries
½ cup coconut milk
½ cup coconut oil
juice of ½ lemon

FOR THE BLUEBERRY COULIS
½ cup frozen blueberries
½ cup pure maple syrup

1. To make the base layer, process all the ingredients in a food processor for 2 to 3 minutes, until the mixture sticks together when you pinch it. Spoon the mixture into an 8-inch springform pan (a square one, if you have it), and press down evenly with the back of the spoon.

2. To make the blueberry layer, process all the ingredients in the food processor for about 5 minutes, or until smooth and creamy; you may need to stop every couple of minutes and scrape down any wayward cashews from the sides of the bowl. Pour the blueberry mixture on top of the base layer, then place in the freezer for 4 hours to set.

3. To make the coulis, combine the blueberries and maple syrup in a saucepan and heat over medium heat, stirring, until the mixture starts to bubble. Reduce the heat to maintain a simmer and cook for 15 minutes. Pour into a bowl and place in the fridge to cool down.

4. Remove the "cheesecake" from the pan and drizzle the coulis over the "cheesecake." Cut into 16 slices and serve. Store any leftovers in a freezerproof container in the freezer for up to 2 months; remove 1 to 2 hours before serving.

COOKIES-AND-CREAM TORTE

I'm really nosy (although I prefer the term "curious"), especially when it comes to what other people get up to in their kitchens (no, not that, I'm talking cooking here). A mommy friend of mine recently had a big dinner party, so when I next caught up with her for coffee (mine's a decaf almond latte, if you're nosy, too), I quizzed her on what she had rustled up for her lucky guests: an amazing three-course dinner, including a decadent cookies-and-cream torte for dessert. Whereupon she challenged me to come up with a healthier version of the torte. You might have guessed from the fact that you're reading this recipe that I'm pretty damn happy with the results. With its baked chocolate cookie base layer, topped with a layer of decadent creamy vanilla flecked with chocolate cookie chunks, it makes the perfect dinner-party dessert!

✳ SERVES 10

FOR THE BASE LAYER AND COOKIE CHUNKS
1¼ cups cacao powder
1 cup ground almonds
½ cup buckwheat flour
6 tablespoons pure maple syrup
5 tablespoons coconut oil, melted,
    plus extra for greasing
5 tablespoons cashew butter (see tip, page 22)

FOR THE FILLING
1 cup raw cashews, soaked in water
    for at least 4 hours, then drained
1 cup chilled full-fat coconut milk (see page 12)
½ cup coconut oil
1 teaspoon pure vanilla extract
7 tablespoons pure maple syrup
cacao nibs
Raw Dark Chocolate (page 31), for drizzling

1. Preheat the oven to 350°F. Grease the bottom of an 8-inch springform pan with coconut oil and line a baking sheet with parchment paper.

2. To make the base layer and cookie chunks, mix together the cacao powder, ground almonds, and buckwheat flour in a mixing bowl. Stir in the maple syrup, melted coconut oil, and cashew butter, then knead until you have a smooth dough. Take two-thirds of the dough and, using a spoon, press it out evenly over the bottom of the prepared pan into a layer about ½ inch thick. Roughly shape the remainder of the dough into about 6 round cookies and place them on the lined baking sheet. Bake for 10 minutes, then remove the cookies from the oven and bake the base layer for 2 minutes more. Remove the base layer from the oven and let cool completely. When the cookies have cooled, pop them into a plastic bag and seal it, then use a rolling pin to smash them into chunks and crumbs.

3. To make the filling, process all the filling ingredients in a food processor until smooth and creamy. Add the smashed cookies to the filling and stir well.

4. Pour the filling on top of the base layer and place in the freezer for at least 4 hours to set. Drizzle with chocolate and cacao nibs, if desired, and serve, or store in a freezerproof container in the freezer for up to 2 months; remove an hour before serving.

MATCHA PISTACHIO COCONUT CREAM TART

Eat your greens, said every mother ever to their children. With pleasure, replied no child ever. These days I count broccoli and kale among my favorite foods, but that definitely wasn't always the case. Luckily, Baby H seems to really like broccoli; kale not so much, but hey, baby steps, right?

You might not want to eat all your vegetables, but if you make this tart, you'll be eating your greens till the cows come home (from eating their greens). It's got a green crust and a green filling without a stalk of broccoli or a leaf of spinach in sight. Eating your greens just got sweeter ...although do still ensure you get your veggies in, too! ✱ SERVES 10

FOR THE TART SHELL
1 cup desiccated coconut
½ cup raw pistachio nuts
1 cup pitted Medjool dates

FOR THE FILLING
¼ cup cacao butter
½ cup pure maple syrup
1 cup coconut milk
1 tablespoon matcha green tea powder

FOR GARNISH (OPTIONAL)
edible rose petals
Raw White Chocolate (page 31, melted)

1. To make the tart shell, process all the tart shell ingredients in a food processor until they form a sticky mixture. Spoon the mixture into an 8-inch pie dish or tart pan and press down with the back of the spoon so that it covers the bottom and sides evenly.

2. To make the filling, melt the cacao butter in a heatproof bowl over a saucepan half-full of gently boiling water over medium heat. Stir in the maple syrup and then the coconut milk and matcha powder until all is well mixed.

3. Pour the filling into the tart shell and place in the fridge for 2 hours to set. Decorate with edible rose petals and drizzle with melted raw white chocolate, if you like, and serve. Store in an airtight container in the fridge for up to 5 days or freeze for up to 2 months.

MINT CHOC CHIP ICE CREAM "CHEESECAKE"

I love growing mint in the garden (although I've learned that it must be kept in a pot because wow, does it spread) for delicious fresh mint teas on tap. Mr. H buys packets of mints by the truckload and never passes up an opportunity to rise to the "After Eight challenge"—if you know, you know. And Baby H seems to like eating her toothpaste rather than brushing her teeth with it. So I had a sneaky feeling that a minty and chocolaty dessert might just prove to be a hit in the House of Hollingsworth. Turns out, I was right; this "cheesecake" was rapidly devoured and received thumbs-up all round. It's also nut-free, as I've used banana instead of cashews in the filling, which you can't really taste due to the strength of the minty flavor.

✳ SERVES 10

FOR THE BASE LAYER
1½ cups desiccated coconut
1½ cups pitted Medjool dates
¼ cup cacao powder
¼ cup cacao nibs
1 tablespoon water, plus more if needed

FOR THE MINT CHOC CHIP LAYER
2 ripe bananas, peeled
1 cup coconut milk
½ cup coconut oil, plus extra for greasing
¼ cup pure maple syrup
½ teaspoon mint extract
½ teaspoon spirulina powder, for coloring (optional)
¼ cup cacao nibs

FOR GARNISH (OPTIONAL)
cacao nibs
raw chocolate (see page 31)
mint leaves

1. Grease an 8-inch springform pan with coconut oil.

2. To make the base layer, process all the base layer ingredients in a food processor until you have a sticky and crumbly mixture.

3. Spoon the mixture into the prepared pan and press down evenly with the back of the spoon. Place in the freezer while you make the mint choc chip layer.

4. To make the mint choc chip layer, process all the ingredients except the cacao nibs in the food processor or a high-speed blender until smooth and creamy—ensure your processor/blender is on the highest setting or the ingredients may not mix together as well. Stir in the cacao nibs.

5. Remove the base layer from the freezer and pour the mint choc chip mixture on top. Place in the freezer overnight to set. Just before serving, garnish with cacao nibs, raw chocolate, and mint leaves, if you like. Store leftovers in a freezerproof container in the freezer for up to 2 months; remove from the freezer 30 minutes before serving.

✳ TOP TIP
Instead of spirulina, you can give the filling a minty-green color using matcha, wheatgrass, or any other green-colored superfood powder, or even a handful of spinach leaves.

This chapter is, in essence, my life story as told through tarts and pies. Does that sound weird? Stay with me and I'll explain why.

Every Friday growing up, we gathered together as a family with my grandparents for dinner—such precious times for which I am very grateful. Each week we would have a delicious main dish and a dessert, usually some sort of pie or tart, with ice cream and fruit salad. Now as an adult (with training wheels on—I'm still learning), I often bring along a tart or pie of some sort to family gatherings. We all have our favorites: my dad, Mr. H, my mother-in-law, and I are all on Team Chocolate; my brother and mom are firm apple pie lovers; my brother-in-law raves about my banoffee pie; and my nieces love my pink vanilla pie, which I'm guessing has something to do with its color.

So coming your way is a pie recipe for every season and every occasion; whether you want something light and fruity for summer or warm and comforting on a wintry day. These recipes are great for entertaining or if you don't want to turn up somewhere empty-handed. They can all be made in advance, travel pretty well (just beware of any sudden braking), and all look quite impressive, too. Oh, and they're all easy as pie to make!

CHAPTER 6
*
TANTALIZING
TARTS & PIES

PINK VELVET VANILLA PIE

I'm definitely a girly girl and adore pink, but there comes a time when it's a bit weird to be dressed head to toe in fifty shades of it. Luckily, there is always food to resort to in fulfilling my pink obsession. In my opinion, pink food is prettier, which means it's tastier, too, and this pink velvet vanilla pie is certainly no exception. I created it for my niece's second birthday party, though she doesn't love pink quite as much as I do, but I'm working on it via her subconscious, as she does love desserts.

This pie looks like it would get top marks at Barbie's bake-off, and boasts a chocolaty, chewy base layer and a super-creamy, light and oh-so-vanilla-y filling. Did I mention it's pink, too? ✳ SERVES 10

FOR THE CRUST
1½ cups raw cashews
1 cup pitted dried dates
½ raw beet, peeled and chopped into small
   chunks or grated
¼ cup cacao powder

FOR THE PIE FILLING
1 cup raw cashews, soaked in water
   for at least 4 hours, then drained
⅔ cup chilled full-fat coconut milk (see page 12)
½ raw beet, peeled and grated
¼ cup coconut oil
¼ cup pure maple syrup
1 teaspoon pure vanilla extract

Raw Dark Chocolate page 31), melted,
   for drizzling (optional)

1. To make the crust, process all the crust ingredients in a food processor for a couple of minutes, or until they form a sticky mixture. Spoon the mixture into an 8-inch pie dish or tart pan and press down with the back of the spoon so that it covers the bottom and sides evenly.

2. To make the filling, process all the ingredients in the food processor or a high-speed blender for about 5 minutes, or until really smooth and creamy. Spoon the filling evenly into the crust and place in the freezer for at least 2 hours to set. Just before slicing and serving, drizzle with melted raw chocolate for extra deliciousness, if you like! Store leftovers in a freezerproof container in the freezer for up to 2 months; remove from the freezer 30 minutes before serving.

SALTED CARAMEL PECAN PIES

I love the idea of Thanksgiving, dedicating a day to spend with friends and family and being thankful for everything we have, and also the concept of a traditional Thanksgiving dinner. Of course, dessert, and in particular, pecan pie, is what makes me most excited. Sometimes, though, it can be hard to practice gratitude among the stresses of everyday life. So here are some things to be grateful for:

Pecan pie—I mean, what an invention. Delicious crunchy pecans + gooey caramel = autumn dessert heaven.

Mini pecan pies—You get to eat all the crust, all the filling and you can feel like a giant in the process.

Raw mini pecan pies—No need to even own or turn on the oven, no fussing around with baking sheets or oven mitts, and no risk of burning your hands.

Now go make these pies—you'll feel truly thankful for it, I promise! ✱ MAKES 6 MINI PIES

FOR THE CRUST
1½ cups gluten-free rolled oats
1½ cups pitted Medjool dates
1 cup pecans
1 teaspoon ground cinnamon
pinch of Himalayan pink salt

FOR THE SALTED CARAMEL PECAN FILLING
1 cup pitted Medjool dates
⅔ cup almond milk (see page 18)
1 cup pecans, plus more for garnish,
   if desired
½ cup cashew butter (see tip, page 22)
pinch of Himalayan pink salt

1. To make the crust, process all the crust ingredients in a food processor until they form a smooth, sticky mixture. Spoon the mixture into six fluted mini pie pans (about 4 inches in diameter) and press down with the back of the spoon so that it covers the bottom and sides evenly. Pop in the fridge while you make the caramel filling.

2. To make the filling, process all the filling ingredients in the food processor for about 5 minutes, or smooth. Spoon the filling evenly into the crusts, then garnish with extra pecans, if you like. Place the pies in the fridge for an hour to set before serving. Store in an airtight container in the fridge for up to 5 days or freeze for up to 2 months.

BANOFFEE PIE

My brother-in-law will tell anyone who will listen that my banoffee pie is the best he has ever tried, which to me is the greatest compliment this dessert could have received. Recently it was his fortieth birthday, so I made him an extra-special one to celebrate.

I love making this banoffee pie for entertaining, as it requires no cooking (so it's great if your oven is busy making a delicious dinner) and can be made in advance, too. It can even be frozen, although I would recommend putting the coconut cream and any final decorations on just before serving. ✳ SERVES 10

FOR THE CRUST
1 cup raw cashews
1 cup pecans
1 cup pitted Medjool dates

FOR THE CARAMEL-BANANA FILLING
1½ cups pitted Medjool dates
1 cup almond milk (see page 18)
2 tablespoons almond butter
2 ripe bananas, plus more for garnish, if desired

FOR THE CREAM
⅔ cup chilled full-fat coconut milk (see page 12)
1 teaspoon pure vanilla extract
½ teaspoon ground cinnamon
2 tablespoons pure maple syrup

1. To make the crust, process all the crust ingredients in a food processor for a couple of minutes, or until they form a crumbly, sticky mixture. Spoon the mixture into an 8-inch fluted pie dish or tart pan and press down with the back of the spoon so that it covers the bottom and sides evenly.

2. To make the caramel-banana filling, process the dates, almond milk, and almond butter in the food processor for about 2 minutes, or until the mixture is all lovely and smooth. Peel the bananas and cut into small slices, put them in a mixing bowl, and stir in the date mixture until well mixed. Spoon the filling evenly into the crust and smooth the surface with the back of the spoon. Place the pie in the freezer for 15 minutes to set a little while you make the cream. (At this stage, you can freeze the pie in a freezerproof container for up to 2 months.)

3. To make the cream, mix together all the ingredients for the cream in a mixing bowl.

4. Remove the pie from the freezer and spoon the cream on top, smoothing it with the back of the spoon to make it nice and even. Store in the fridge until ready to serve, up to 3 days. If you fancy giving your pie a little jazzy decoration, sprinkle over some chopped nuts and grated chocolate or chop a banana or two into slices and arrange on top before serving.

MY CLASSIC CHOCOLATE MOUSSE TART

Chocolate mousse and me have had a thing going on for decades. Growing up, I loved the little pots of it you could get from the supermarket, but the best one I've ever had was in a restaurant where it was served in a glass with some sort of raw chocolate brownie at the bottom. So that's what I'm aiming at here, but in a tart. The combination of silky-smooth chocolate mousse with a crunchy-chewy tart base is simply out of this world. There's no denying that this tart, like Julia Roberts in *Pretty Woman*, is definitely a little bit sexy, which makes it the perfect end to a date night candlelit dinner. That said, you don't need to be on a date night to enjoy it, and it's also nut-free, so you really have no excuse not to go for it. ✳ SERVES 10

FOR THE BASE LAYER
½ cup buckwheat groats
1 cup pitted Medjool dates
1 cup gluten-free rolled oats
½ cup cacao powder
½ cup water, plus more if needed

FOR THE FILLING
2 ripe bananas, peeled
1 cup pitted Medjool dates
1 ripe avocado, halved, pitted, and peeled
3 tablespoons cacao powder
1 tablespoon coconut oil

cacao nibs, for garnish (optional)

1. Preheat the oven to 350°F.

2. To make the base layer, spread the buckwheat groats out on a baking sheet and toast in the oven for 10 minutes, then let cool.

3. Transfer the groats to a food processor, add the dates, oats, cacao powder, and water, and process for 2 minutes, or until sticky, adding a little more water if the mixture is not sticking together enough.

4. Spoon the mixture into an 8-inch pie dish or tart pan and press down with the back of the spoon so that it covers the bottom evenly.

5. To make the filling, process all the filling ingredients in a food processor for about 3 minutes, or until creamy. Spoon the filling evenly over the base layer, then garnish with cacao nibs, if you like, and place in the freezer for 2 hours to set. Transfer to a plate and store in the fridge until ready to serve, up to 3 days, or store in the freezer in a freezerproof container for up to a month.

APPLE OF MY EYE PIE

When my brother moved to Australia for a couple of years with his now wife, it felt like a lifetime away. Everyone knows that the way to a man's heart is through his stomach, so I thought if I made a tempting enough version of his all-time favorite dessert, apple pie, then just maybe he might consider coming back a little earlier. When I sent him photos of my creation, he asked me to send some Down Under, and before I knew it, he'd booked a plane ticket home. Coincidence? I think not.

Apple pie is popular with almost everyone— you just can't go wrong with it. I don't think there is any other fruit that "pie-ifies" quite so well. ✶ SERVES 10

FOR THE PIE CRUST

⅔ cup coconut oil, plus extra
   for greasing and (melted)
   for brushing 2 cups gluten-free rolled
   oats
2 cups buckwheat flour,
   plus extra for dusting
1 teaspoon ground cinnamon
½ cup pure maple syrup
4 to 6 tablespoons water, as needed

FOR THE FILLING

4 cups peeled, cored, and
   thinly sliced apples (any variety)
1 tablespoon pure maple syrup
½ teaspoon ground cinnamon

Vanilla Cashew Ice Cream
   (page 29) or Coconut
   Whipped Cream (page 26),
   for serving

1. To make the pie crust, preheat the oven to 350°F. Grease an 8-inch pie dish or flan pan with coconut oil.

2. Process the oats in a food processor or high-speed blender for about 1 minute, or until they form a fine flour. Tip into a mixing bowl and stir in the buckwheat flour and cinnamon. Rub the coconut oil into the dry ingredients with your fingertips to create a bread-crumb-like texture, then mix in the maple syrup. Stir in the water, a tablespoon at a time, until the dough can be rolled into a big ball (but be careful not to add too much water, as you don't want the dough to be too sticky).

3. Divide the dough into two equal-sized balls. On a flour-dusted work surface, roll one ball out with a rolling pin until it's about 10 inches in diameter, then use it to line the bottom and sides of the prepared pan and trim any excess dough from around the rim.

4. To make the filling, place the apple slices in a mixing bowl with the maple syrup and cinnamon and toss well so all the apples are evenly coated. Then lay them out evenly in the dough-lined pan.

5. Roll out the remaining dough into a round slightly smaller than before, then cut it into ¾-inch-wide strips. Lay half the strips out horizontally over the pie and the other half vertically to create a lattice.

6. Brush the top of the pie with some melted coconut oil and bake for 30 minutes, or until golden brown on top. Eat it hot, with a big scoop of homemade ice cream or a dollop of coconut whipped cream, or let it cool for a couple of hours and enjoy it cold.

COOKIE PIZZA PIE

You might know the song lyric, "When the moon hits your eye like a big pizza pie, that's amore," but do you know the lesser-quoted second line, "When this cookie pizza pie hits your lips like a lunar eclipse, you'll want more, eh"? OK, so maybe I made that up, but what I can tell you is that sweet pizzas are the next big thing.

When I was seventeen, twenty of my friends and I went to Magaluf on the island of Majorca for a crazy week of foam parties, buckets of questionable alcohol, and sunburn. Across the road from our hotel, there was an Italian restaurant serving great cheap pizza, including a "banana pizza," which at that time was such a crazy idea, we found it nothing short of hilarious.

Here I am, many years later, eating humble (cookie pizza) pie. Cookies are good, but one big giant cookie is even better, and topped with jelly, chocolate, and all the fruit, we are talking serious dessert goals. To the owner of Diabolo Pizza in Palmanova, I doff my hat to you, for you, my friend, are one smart cookie. ✳ SERVES 8

FOR THE COOKIE PIZZA CRUST
1 cup gluten-free rolled oats
1¼ cups ground almonds
6 tablespoons pure maple syrup
3 tablespoons coconut oil, melted
3 tablespoons almond milk (see page 18)

FOR THE PIZZA TOPPINGS
Berry Chia Jelly (page 26), made with strawberries, or Hazelnut Chocolate Spread (page 20)
¼ cup shaved Raw White Chocolate (page 31)
sliced fresh fruit
¼ cup raw chocolate nonpareils
fresh mint

1. Preheat the oven to 350°F. Line an 8-inch round cake pan or baking sheet with parchment paper.

2. To make the base layer, process the oats in a food processor or high-speed blender for about 30 seconds, or until they form a flour. Transfer to a mixing bowl and stir in the ground almonds. Add the maple syrup, melted coconut oil, and almond milk and stir to combine, then use your hands to gather the mixture into a big ball of dough. Place the dough on the bottom of the prepared pan and use your hands to flatten it into a round about ¾ inch thick, then bake for 15 minutes. Let cool completely before you add the toppings.

3. How you decorate your cookie pizza is up to you, but my favorite combination is a smothering of jelly, some white chocolate shavings, sliced fruit, and maybe a sneaky chocolate nonpareil or two, plus a sprinkling of fresh mint just to complete the picture.

PERFECT BERRY PARFAIT GRANOLA CUPS

My go-to breakfast in my old cafeteria at work was a mountain of Greek yogurt, lots of berries, and some very sugary granola—in essence, a breakfast parfait—and the company I worked for was a French one. So, with *parfait* meaning "perfect" in French, it was literally the perfect breakfast. Unfortunately, how I felt afterward wasn't so perfect, and although that improved when I gave up eating it, my mornings beginning with porridge made with water felt far from perfect.

These granola cups are an ingenious invention, if I do say so myself. You can fill them with whatever you like, and you don't need either a bowl or a spoon to eat them with. You can even eat them one-handed, which for busy people always trying to do a hundred things at once, is a real bonus. Fill these with chopped berries and coconut yogurt for the ultimate in parfait perfection.

✳ MAKES ABOUT 10 CUPS

FOR THE GRANOLA CUPS
1 cup gluten-free rolled oats
1 ripe banana, peeled and mashed
2 tablespoons pure maple syrup
½ teaspoon ground cinnamon

FOR THE BERRY PARFAIT
½ cup coconut yogurt
about ½ cup chopped fresh berries (I like strawberries and blueberries)

1. Preheat the oven to 350°F.

2. To make the granola cups, stir together all the ingredients for the granola cups in a mixing bowl until well mixed.

3. Spoon the mixture into a silicone mini muffin pan (or a regular mini-muffin pan lined with paper liners) and press over the bottom and up the sides to form mini tart shells. Bake for 10 minutes, or until lightly golden. Let cool. You can freeze the unfilled cups at this point for up to a month.

4. To assemble the parfaits, fill the granola cups with the coconut yogurt and chopped berries.

MOJITO KEY LIME PIE

When I was younger, I once got very drunk on mojitos, so after that I avoided them, until last summer when Mr. H and I went on vacation to Miami and Cuba. We spent a couple of days in a cute little hotel in South Beach, partied with the locals on the Fourth of July, and found the most delicious key lime pie, that Floridian delicacy, which I vowed to re-create when we got home. We then boarded a plane to Cuba, only to circle the Havana airport for an hour due to a storm, before returning to Miami to refuel and then start again. After that, I was ready for a drink. We sat in our hotel lobby listening to beautiful live music, dancing with Baby H, and sipping mojitos (mine minus the sugar), and suddenly all the mile-high trauma was forgotten.

This dessert is a Cuban twist on the classic, with the tangy lime and creamy coconut filling given a refreshing minty boost. It's a summer staple in my home, as it tastes just like the cocktail in a dessert! * SERVES 10

FOR THE CRUST
coconut oil, for greasing
1½ cups desiccated coconut
1 cup pecans
½ cup pitted Medjool dates

FOR THE FILLING
½ cup coconut milk
1 ripe avocado, halved, pitted, and peeled
juice of 1 lime
6 tablespoons coconut oil
½ cup pure maple syrup
½ teaspoon mint extract
pinch of Himalayan pink salt

TO GARNISH
fresh mint
1 lime, cut into slices
dessicated coconut

1. To make the crust, grease an 8-inch pie dish or tart pan with coconut oil.

2. Process all the crust ingredients in a food processor until sticky. Spoon the mixture into the prepared pan and press down with the back of the spoon so it covers the bottom and sides evenly.

3. To make the filling, process all the filling ingredients in the food processor or a high-speed blender for 5 minutes, or until smooth and creamy. Spoon into the crust and freeze for 4 hours until set.

4. Remove the pie from the freezer an hour before serving and garnish with the fresh mint, lime, and desiccated coconut. Store any leftovers in a freezerproof container in the freezer (to stop the avocado from browning) for up to 2 months.

"JAFFA" CHOCOLATE-ORANGE TARTLETS

Full moon, half moon, total eclipse! Jaffa cakes are a quintessentially British treat, and for many people, they're a go-to when it comes to nostalgic comfort eating. Mr. H is one of the biggest Jaffa cake fans I know, and he was bitterly disappointed when, upon visiting Jaffa in Israel, there was not a cake to be seen. Freshly squeezed orange juice helped him ease the pain, but it didn't really fill the void.

These tartlets are totally scrumptious and the perfect teatime accompaniment. They've got a cakey base covered with a gooey orange caramel, finished off with delicious raw chocolate. They're basically just like Jaffa cakes only bigger. Sounds good, doesn't it?!

✳ MAKES ABOUT 6 TARTLETS (OR 1 LARGE TART)

FOR THE TARTLET SHELLS
¼ cup coconut oil,
   plus extra for greasing 2 cups
ground almonds
½ cup buckwheat flour
¼ cup cashew butter (see
   tip on page 22)
6 Medjool dates, pitted
½ cup pure maple syrup
¼ cup water

FOR THE ORANGE CARAMEL
½ cup pitted Medjool dates
finely grated zest of ½ orange
½ cup cashew butter (see
   tip, page 22)
½ cup classic almond milk
   (see page 18)
pinch of Himalayan pink salt
½ teaspoon ground turmeric,
   for coloring (optional)

FOR THE CHOCOLATE TOPPING
½ cup coconut oil
¼ cup cacao powder
3 tablespoons pure maple syrup
pinch of Himalayan pink salt

finely grated orange zest, for garnish

1. Preheat the oven to 350°F. Grease six 4-inch tartlet pans (or one large tart pan, about 9 inches in diameter) with coconut oil.

2. To make the tartlet shells, process all the ingredients in a food processor until they form a sticky dough. Divide the dough into six pieces, then press each piece into one of the prepared tartlet pans (or the large tart pan) so that it covers the bottom and sides evenly. Bake for 10 minutes (or a few more minutes, if making one large tart) and let cool.

3. To make the orange caramel, process all the ingredients in the food processor or high-speed blender until a sticky caramel forms. Spread evenly into the cooled tartlet shells, ensuring you leave a little room at the top for the topping.

4. To make the topping, melt the coconut oil in a heatproof bowl over a saucepan half-full of gently boiling water over medium heat, then remove from the heat and stir in the cacao powder, maple syrup, and salt until you have a smooth and glossy chocolate mixture.

5. Either drizzle the topping over the tarts or spoon it evenly onto the orange caramel and then place the tartlets in the fridge for 15 minutes to set the chocolate topping. Serve immediately, sprinkled with orange zest, or store in the fridge in an airtight container for up to 5 days or freeze for up to 2 months.

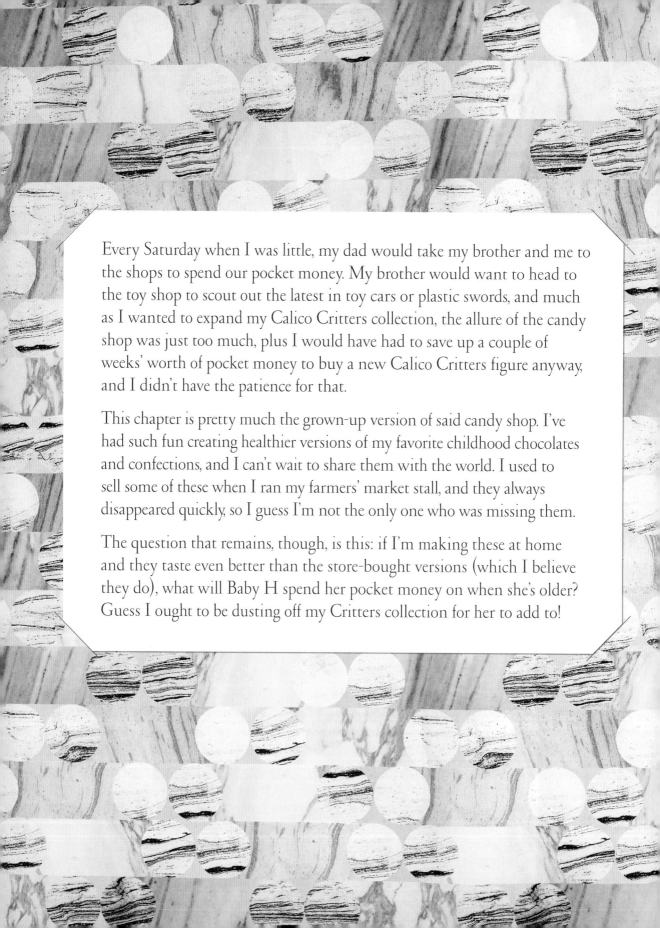

Every Saturday when I was little, my dad would take my brother and me to the shops to spend our pocket money. My brother would want to head to the toy shop to scout out the latest in toy cars or plastic swords, and much as I wanted to expand my Calico Critters collection, the allure of the candy shop was just too much, plus I would have had to save up a couple of weeks' worth of pocket money to buy a new Calico Critters figure anyway, and I didn't have the patience for that.

This chapter is pretty much the grown-up version of said candy shop. I've had such fun creating healthier versions of my favorite childhood chocolates and confections, and I can't wait to share them with the world. I used to sell some of these when I ran my farmers' market stall, and they always disappeared quickly, so I guess I'm not the only one who was missing them.

The question that remains, though, is this: if I'm making these at home and they taste even better than the store-bought versions (which I believe they do), what will Baby H spend her pocket money on when she's older? Guess I ought to be dusting off my Critters collection for her to add to!

CHAPTER 7

*

SERIOUSLY MOREISH CONFECTIONERY & CHOCOLATES

PEANUT BUTTER CUPS

I've always loved peanut butter, but it was on a trip to the US about ten years ago that I first discovered peanut butter cups. I had gone to the States for the summer on my own, and being without parental guidance for the first time, I ended up pretty much eating my weight in these beauties. I just couldn't believe my luck in finding my two favorite foods ever combined in one delicious treat! On my return to the UK, I crammed as many packages as I could into my suitcase, and was delighted when, a few years later, they turned up in shops over here, too. These homemade ones are equally (if not more) tasty! * MAKES 18 CUPS

½ cup cacao butter
3 tablespoons cacao powder
3 tablespoons pure maple syrup
3 tablespoons peanut butter (see page 21)
peanut halves, for garnish (optional)

1. Melt the cacao butter in a heatproof bowl over a saucepan half-full of boiling water over medium heat, then stir in the cacao powder and maple syrup. Pour half the mixture into 18 mini cupcake liners, then place them in the fridge for 15 minutes to set.

2. Remove from the fridge and spoon ½ teaspoon of the peanut butter into the center of each one, then pour the remaining chocolate mixture on top (rewarm it if needed) so the peanut butter is completely covered.

3. Return to the fridge for about 30 minutes, then top each with half a peanut, if desired, and dig in! Store in an airtight container in the fridge for up to 2 weeks.

RAWLOS

Do you love someone enough to give them your last one? This posed quite a conundrum when I was little for both me and my dad , a fellow chocoholic, despite me being the world's biggest daddy's girl and the apple of his eye, as we both always felt the pain of parting with that final Rolo in the packet.

At my high school, every Valentine's Day the boys school next door would sell "last Rolos," which pupils could get anonymously delivered to the lucky recipients of their choosing. I don't think I ever received any—braces, home hair highlighting disasters, and just general teenage awkwardness meant I wasn't a prime target for such romantic gestures.

So to save anyone else the trouble of my aforementioned dilemmas and teenage angst, I've created these (even yummier) Rawlos. Plus, they are so simple that if you think you're about to get down to your last one, you can quickly make some more. Crisis averted! ✳ MAKES ABOUT 20 RAWLOS

½ cup pitted dried dates
¼ cup almond milk (see page 18)
½ tablespoon almond butter, or any other nut or seed butter
¼ teaspoon pure vanilla extract
1 batch Dark Raw Chocolate (page 31)

1. Process all the ingredients except the chocolate in a food processor or high-speed blender for a couple of minutes, or until a smooth, sticky, gooey caramel forms. Spoon into a bowl and pop in the freezer for 30 minutes to set slightly.

2. Make the raw chocolate following the recipe on page 31, then spoon a little into a silicone chocolate mold (or an ice cube tray or mini cupcake liners) to fill by about one-third. Place in the fridge for 15 minutes to set, keeping the remainder of the chocolate melted.

3. Remove the caramel from the freezer and the chocolate from the fridge, and use a teaspoon to pop a small amount of caramel into the middle of each individual mold so that they are about two-thirds full, but try to avoid the caramel going into the edges. Then pour over more of the melted chocolate so that the molds are full and the caramel is completely covered. Return to the fridge for 1 hour more to set completely before you dig in. Store in an airtight container in the fridge for up to 2 weeks.

ALSO PICTURED: MELT-IN-THE-MIDDLE CHOCOLATE TRUFFLES see following page for recipe

MELT-IN-THE-MIDDLE CHOCOLATE TRUFFLES

One Christmas, Santa kindly delivered to me a big box of Lindor truffles. When it comes to Christmas different rules apply, so I sat in bed opening the rest of my gifts while unwrapping the truffles, one by one. I got a little distracted, and before I knew it, I had eaten half the box and felt slightly sick! These truffles are my take on those delicious treats, but be warned, it's just as hard to restrain yourself with them. Their melt-in-the-mouth silky chocolate center, covered with a delicious raw chocolate shell are irresistible. So perhaps I should add a disclaimer: do not eat while distracted! * MAKES 15 TRUFFLES

FOR THE TRUFFLE CENTERS
½ cup cacao butter
5 tablespoons cacao powder
3 tablespoons pure maple syrup
½ cup almond butter
½ cup coconut milk
pinch of Himalayan pink salt

FOR THE DARK CHOCOLATE COATING
¼ cup cacao butter
2 tablespoons cacao powder
2 tablespoons pure maple syrup
pinch of Himalayan pink salt

1. To make the truffle centers, melt the cacao butter in a heatproof bowl over a saucepan half-full of boiling water over medium heat. Remove from the heat, add the other ingredients, and stir until smooth and creamy. Pour into a silicone mold (or an ice cube tray or mini cupcake liners) and freeze for 2 hours to set.

2. To make the coating, melt the cacao butter as above, then stir in the other ingredients. Remove the truffles from the molds, then dip them, one by one, into the coating. Once they've all been dipped, dip them again, until you have used up the coating mixture. Store in an airtight container in the fridge for up to 1 week.

PHARAOH MINT CHOC CRUNCH BARS

Going way back into my childhood, I used to love an Aero. And then they came out with a few different flavors and I fell head over heels for the mint version. That combination of minty + chocolaty + bubbles had me obsessed. But those bubbles in the chocolate—anyone who knows how they do it, please let me know! I once tried using one of Baby H's straws to blow bubbles into my chocolate, but it didn't end well and I had a whole lot of cleaning up to do afterward.

It's OK, though, because I discovered that crunchy buckwheat + chocolate + mint = the next best thing, or, dare I say it, perhaps even better? Well, I do dare (*audere est facere*, for all my Spurs fans out there), so prepare to be amazed. My Pharaoh bars, named as such because they're the kings of the chocolate world, should be included in every food pyramid! * MAKES 8 BARS

½ cup coconut oil, melted
½ cup cacao powder
¼ cup pure maple syrup
2 drops of pure peppermint extract
pinch of Himalayan pink salt
½ cup buckwheat groats, toasted and cooled (see page 108)

1. Stir together all the ingredients except the toasted buckwheat in a mixing bowl until smooth and glossy, then stir in the buckwheat.

2. Pour the mixture into an 8-well silicone mold or a loaf pan lined with parchment paper. Place in the freezer for an hour to set, then remove from the mold or cut into bars with a sharp knife (if you've used a loaf pan). Store in an airtight container in the fridge for up to 2 weeks.

"SNICK" ME ANOTHER PEANUT CARAMEL BARS

Every week, my lovely namesake and kitchen angel Emma and I make over 150 of these bars. That's almost eight thousand a year, which coincidentally is about how many I think I've eaten since I created them. How's that for quality control?

These initially came about after a huge Christmas Day meal with Mr. H's family when a box of mixed chocolate candy bars began to circulate. Not for me, I said, but the usual suspects dug in. The classic favorites disappeared quickly, and left behind were all the Snickers. It took everything I had not to join in and fish them out, but I knew I would feel like garbage the next day if I did. So as soon as I got back home, I got in the kitchen and came up with these to satisfy my craving. I've never looked back!

✳ MAKES 12 BARS

FOR THE BASE LAYER
1 cup gluten-free rolled oats
1 cup ground almonds
2 tablespoons coconut oil
¼ cup pure maple syrup

FOR THE PEANUT CARAMEL LAYER
⅓ cup pitted Medjool dates
½ cup peanut butter (see page 21)
½ cup almond milk (see page 18)
1 tablespoon coconut oil
pinch of Himalayan pink salt
¼ cup raw blanched peanuts, roasted (see page 21) and roughly chopped

FOR THE CHOCOLATE TOPPING
¼ cup coconut oil, melted
¼ cup cacao powder
¼ cup pure maple syrup
¼ cup peanut butter (see page 21)
pinch of Himalayan pink salt

1. To make the base layer, process the oats in a food processor or high-speed blender for about 1 minute, or until they form a fine flour. Then add the other ingredients and process for a minute more, or until the mixture becomes a sticky ball. Spoon the mixture into a 12-well silicone mold and use your fingers to press it down evenly.

2. To make the peanut caramel layer, process all the ingredients except the peanuts in a food processor for about 2 minutes, or until smooth, then stir in the peanuts. Spoon evenly on top of the base layer and place in the freezer for 4 hours to set.

3. To make the topping, mix together all the ingredients in a mixing bowl until smooth and thick. Remove the bars from the freezer and spoon the topping onto the peanut caramel layer, then return to the freezer for 30 minutes more to set. Store in an airtight container in the fridge for up to 3 days or freeze for up to 2 months.

✳ TOP TIP

If you don't have a silicone mold, you can use a rectangular baking pan or loaf pan lined with parchment paper instead, then use a sharp knife to cut into bars.

HAZELNUT RAW NO-SHARES

These are a delicious twist on the classic gold foil–wrapped hazelnut chocolates. You know, the ones where they're stacked in a giant pyramid in the ad. When I started running my market stall, I had visions of selling these in a similar way, gold foil and all. Turned out that they aren't very easy to stack, and they were way too big to wrap in the gold foils I spent ages sourcing!

This version, in my opinion, tastes even better than the original. I still can't make them into a pyramid, but I'm over that now (kind of). ✷ MAKES ABOUT 12 BALLS

1 cup hazelnuts, plus an extra hazelnut
  for each ball
1 cup pitted Medjool dates
2 tablespoons cacao powder

FOR THE CHOCOLATE COATING
½ cup cacao butter or coconut oil, melted
¼ cup pure maple syrup
3 tablespoons cacao powder
¼ cup chopped toasted hazelnuts
  (you can buy these prechopped and
  toasted in most supermarkets)

1. Process the hazelnuts, dates, and cacao powder in a food processor until the ingredients start to stick together. Roll into 12 balls with a hazelnut at the center of each, then place in the freezer for an hour.

2. To make the coating, mix together all the ingredients except the hazelnuts, then stir in the hazelnuts.

3. Remove the balls from the freezer and, one by one, roll them in the coating, then place on a plate. Once you've coated them all, coat them again, until you have used up the coating. Place in the fridge for 10 minutes to set (the coating will set quicker the longer the balls have been in the freezer). Store in an airtight container in the fridge for up to 2 weeks.

TAHINI SALTED CARAMEL FUDGE

There is always tahini in my fridge. Where I live there are lots of amazing international grocery shops, and one of them sells huge jars of the most delicious tahini. I go through it like it's going out of fashion (which I can assure you it isn't), drizzling it on my roasted vegetables, using it in hummus, and adding it to lime, tamari, and sesame oil to make the best dressings.

But it isn't just for savory stuff, oh no. When I get requests for nut-free cakes or brownies, I often use tahini as a nut butter replacement. I created this fudge for decorating one showstopper of a nut-free cake, and since then I've been totally obsessed with it. It consists of only four ingredients and is the perfect mix of sweet, salty and savory.
✷ MAKES 12 SMALL SQUARES

½ cup tahini
2½ tablespoons cacao butter, melted
2½ tablespoons pure maple syrup
pinch of Himalayan pink salt

1. Stir all the ingredients together well in a mixing bowl until you have a thick, creamy mixture. Pour into a silicone chocolate mold or a shallow 8-inch square baking pan lined with parchment paper and place in the freezer for 2 hours to set.

2. Remove from the molds or cut into 12 small squares with a sharp knife if you've used a baking pan. Store in an airtight container in the fridge for up to 1 week.

RAW FROSTED GEMSTONES

Back in the '90s, the world was a very different place. The music scene was dominated by girl groups and boy bands in matching outfits, rhyming "baby" with "crazy" in their lyrics, crop tops and platform sneakers were the height of fashion, and at kid's parties the spread included more often than not of little cookies with icing-flower tops.

What goes around comes around, and 99.9 percent of said pop bands seem to have had a comeback in the last five years (much to my delight), so back are the platform boots and midriff-baring clothes (not so much my style anymore), and I'm bringing you a new and updated version of those pastel-toned party snacks. These require no baking, so you don't have to wait around for them to cool before you can frost them, which means more time to dance around to cheesy pop tunes in your platform sneakers.

✶ MAKES ABOUT 30 GEMSTONES

FOR THE COOKIE BASES
1 cup ground almonds
⅔ cup pitted Medjool dates
½ teaspoon pure vanilla extract

FOR THE FROSTING
⅔ cup chilled full-fat coconut milk (see page 12)
½ cup cacao butter, melted
3 tablespoons pure maple syrup
1 tablespoon coconut flour

OPTIONAL NATURAL COLORINGS
½ teaspoon cacao powder
½ teaspoon beet or pink pitaya
½ teaspoon ground turmeric
¼ teaspoon spirulina or wheatgrass powder
juice of 1 blueberry

1. To make the cookie bases, process all the ingredients in a food processor for 2 to 3 minutes, until they form a sticky mixture.

2. Shape the mixture into about 30 small balls (each about the size of a marble) and flatten them into discs. Pop them on a plate and place in the freezer while you make the frosting.

3. To make the frosting, stir together all the frosting ingredients in a mixing bowl. To create the different-colored frostings, grab a couple more bowls, spoon about 2 tablespoons of the frosting into each bowl, and stir a different natural coloring of your choice into each one.

4. Spoon one icing color into a piping bag fitted with a large star tip and carefully squeeze it onto some of the cookies. Repeat for each different-colored icing you are using. Store in an airtight container in the fridge for up to 3 days or freeze for up to 1 month.

MUTINY ON THE . . . COCONUT SLICE

I actually first created these with my mother-in-law in mind, as she absolutely loves Bounty bars. They were such a hit that I knew I was onto something, so I added them to my menu. They have since become one of my top-selling raw desserts.

I sometimes make them in a little heart-shaped mold and sprinkle desiccated coconut and rose petals on top so that they look as appetizing as they taste, and they always sell out like hot cakes. Or should I say, cold cakes, which is my dad's (bad) joke, by the way. Try experimenting with whatever shape mold you have. If you're a coconut and chocolate lover, then these are for you. ✳ MAKES 16 SLICES

FOR THE BASE LAYER
1½ cups desiccated coconut
1 cup pitted Medjool dates
1 cup ground almonds
2 tablespoons cacao powder
2 tablespoons water, or more if needed

FOR THE FILLING
6 tablespoons pure maple syrup
¼ cup coconut milk
¼ cup coconut oil, melted
2 cups desiccated coconut

FOR THE TOPPING
½ cup coconut oil, melted
6 tablespoons cacao powder
6 tablespoons pure maple syrup

1. To make the base layer, process all the ingredients in a food processor for 2 to 3 minutes, adding a little extra water if needed to make the mixture sticky. Spoon the mixture into a shallow 8-inch square baking pan lined with parchment paper, or use a silicone mold in the shape of your choice, and press down evenly with the back of the spoon. Set aside.

2. To make the filling, mix together all the ingredients except the coconut in a mixing bowl, then stir in the coconut. Spoon on top of the base layer and press down evenly with the back of the spoon, then place in the freezer for 4 hours to set.

3. To make the topping, stir together all the ingredients for the topping in a mixing bowl.

4. Remove the bars from the freezer and pour the topping evenly over the top. Place in the fridge for 10 minutes to set, then cut into 16 slices or remove from the mold to serve. Store an airtight container in the fridge for up to 2 weeks or freeze for 2 months.

It was only when we moved into the house we live in now just after our wedding that I really got into using my oven. Having previously been occupied by the same family since it had been built over a hundred years ago, the house had no central heating, and I don't think the kitchen (or bathroom) had ever been updated. But that was what Mr. H and I loved about the place—it was a project. In the interests of saving a bit of dough, we tried to do as much of the revamping as we could ourselves, but some things are better left to the professionals, so we had a brand-spanking-new kitchen installed for us, featuring a shiny new oven.

After over a month of my "kitchen" being a table in the hall, complete with my slow cooker, Vitamix, and electric kettle, I was itching to get to grips with that oven. And so I roasted nuts and baked cookies, cakes, and crumbles like there was no tomorrow.

In this chapter, I share with you the most adored and enjoyed bakes that came out of my newly beloved oven for you to indulge in, too. So fire up your oven and give it some lovin'.

CHAPTER 8

*

FIRE UP THE OVEN... CAKES & LOAVES

BLUEBERRY AND VANILLA CAKE

Baby H absolutely adores blueberries and calls them "bwees," a name that has stuck, so it's not uncommon for Mr. H or I to text each other to "pick up some more bwees" on the other one's way home, because lord have mercy should we run out. Consequently, I always err on the side of caution, so when we have built up a surplus and they are heading toward the wrong side of their best-before date, I grab the excuse to bake (though I know I could freeze them, too). And blueberries lend themselves very well to cake-baking, as they balance sweetness with a delicious tartness. They also go amazingly well with the flavor of vanilla. Blueberries are rich in antioxidants, so this cake not only tastes good but does you good, too. ✳ MAKES 1 CAKE (ABOUT 10 SLICES)

3 cups ground almonds
1 cup buckwheat flour
¼ cup coconut oil, melted
4 flaxseed "eggs" (see page 13)
1 cup pure maple syrup
1 tablespoon pure vanilla extract
1 cup almond milk (see page 18)
1 cup blueberries, plus extra for garnish
Coconut Whipped Cream (page 26), for filling and frosting

1. Preheat the oven to 350°F. Line two 8-inch round cake pans with parchment paper.

2. Mix together the ground almonds and buckwheat flour in a mixing bowl. Add the melted coconut oil, flaxseed "eggs," maple syrup, vanilla, and almond milk and stir together well, then fold in the blueberries.

3. Spoon the mixture equally into the lined cake pans and bake for 30 minutes, or until lightly golden.

4. Let the cakes cool in the tin, then remove and spread or pipe the coconut whipped cream on the top of each cake and place layer on top of the other. Decorate with extra blueberries. Store in an airtight container in the fridge for up to 3 days or freeze for up to 2 months.

SPICY 'N' SWEET CHAI BREAKFAST MUFFINS

Before Baby H came along, Mr. H and I went on the most incredible trip to India. We both fell in love with the country— the noise, the sights, the smells, and, of course, the food. Our tour guide took us to authentic restaurants and cafés, and one day he stopped by the side of a dusty road to get us a chai. Creamy, sweet, spicy, and rich, it was a little taste of heaven.

I was desperate to get a chai recipe in this book, and breakfast muffins work really well with all the spices. Instead of sugar, I've used pure maple syrup and juicy dates, and I've replaced the creamy dairy milk with almond milk and almond butter. These are such a breakfast game-changer!

✳ MAKES 12 MUFFINS

FOR THE CHAI SPICE
1 tablespoon ground cinnamon
1 tablespoon ground ginger
½ teaspoon ground cloves
½ teaspoon ground cardamom

1½ cups ground almonds
1 cup gluten-free rolled oats
½ cup almond butter or Coconut
   Vanilla Almond Butter (page 22)
⅓ cup almond milk (see page 18)
½ cup pure maple syrup
6 Medjool dates, pitted and chopped into chunks
coconut yogurt, for topping (optional)

1. Preheat the oven to 350°F. Line a 12-well muffin tin with paper liners.

2. Stir together all the ingredients for the chai spice in a mixing bowl, then add the ground almonds and oats and stir to combine. Mix in the almond butter, almond milk, and maple syrup until evenly combined. Finally, add the dates and stir in well.

3. Spoon the mixture evenly into the prepared muffin tin and bake for 35 minutes, or until golden on top. Serve warm with coconut yogurt or let cool, store in an airtight container at room temperature, and enjoy throughout the week! Or freeze for up to 2 months.

✳ TOP TIP
To chop the dates easily, snip them into chunks using kitchen scissors.

CHOCOLATE FUDGE SWEET POTATO MUFFINS

Chocolate muffins have been my brother's favorite breakfast for as long as I can remember, and our mom's been buying them for him on special occasions for just as long. Now that we've all gotten a little healthier in my family, he doesn't have them quite so often, but when he goes to stay with our mom she'll still buy him a package of muffins as a treat.

I also used to be partial to the odd chocolate muffin, so I wanted to create my own version to carry on the tradition. Since my brother's wife is allergic to bananas, I devised this banana-free recipe so that she can enjoy them, too. Sweet potatoes proved to be the perfect banana alternative, as they make the muffins super moist and yummy without compromising the flavor.

✱ MAKES 8 MUFFINS

1 sweet potato, peeled and chopped into small chunks (about 130g or 1 cup)
½ cup gluten-free rolled oats
1 cup cacao powder
½ cup ground almonds
1 cup pitted Medjool dates
240ml (1 cup almond milk (see page 18)
2 flaxseed "eggs" (see page 13)
¼ cup coconut oil
raw chocolate (whatever variety you prefer, see page 31), melted, for garnish (optional)

1. Preheat the oven to 350°F. Line eight wells of a muffin tin with paper liners.

2. Place the sweet potato in a saucepan, cover with water, and cook for 15 to 20 minutes over medium heat until completely soft. Drain and set aside.

3. Process the oats in a food processor or high-speed blender for about 1 minute, or until they form a fine flour. Transfer to a mixing bowl and add the cacao powder and ground almonds; stir well. Add the sweet potato and mash well, then stir in the dates, almond milk, flaxseed "eggs," and coconut oil until smooth.

4. Divide the mixture evenly among the lined wells of the muffin tin and bake for 30 to 35 minutes, until a skewer inserted into the center of a muffin comes out clean. Let cool for a couple of minutes before you dig in, or garnish with melted raw chocolate if you fancy an extra chocolate fix! Store in an airtight container in the fridge for up to 5 days or freeze for 2 months.

✱ TOP TIP
If you want to turn these into cupcakes, make a batch of my Four-ingredient Chocolate Frosting (see page 24) and pipe it on top.

CINNAMON AND RAISIN LOAF

Sometimes I don't even have time to find matching socks in the morning, let alone make something healthy for breakfast, which is where this loaf comes in. I make it over the weekend so that we can have it for breakfast on busy mornings during the week. Don't be fooled by the cake-like exterior of this loaf, as it's full of wonderful, tummy-loving ingredients. So not only does it taste like heaven on a plate, but it will also keep you well fueled until your next meal. Or midmorning, whichever comes first. * MAKES 1 LOAF (8 LARGE SLICES)

3 tablespoons coconut oil, melted, plus extra for greasing
2 cups gluten-free rolled oats
1 cup buckwheat flour
2 tablespoons chia seeds
2 tablespoons ground cinnamon
1 ripe banana, peeled and mashed
1¼ cups unsweetened almond milk (see page 18; omit the date)
½ cup pure maple syrup
⅓ cup raisins

FOR THE CINNAMON-MAPLE DRIZZLE
2 tablespoons pure maple syrup
1 tablespoon ground cinnamon

1. Preheat the oven to 350°F. Grease a 4 by 6-inch loaf pan with coconut oil or line it with parchment paper.

2. Process the oats in a food processor or high-speed blender for about 30 seconds, or until they form a flour. Mix with the buckwheat flour, chia seeds, and cinnamon in a mixing bowl. Add the banana, almond milk, maple syrup, and melted coconut oil and mix together well. Finally, stir in the raisins.

3. Spoon the mixture into the prepared loaf pan and bake for about 40 minutes, or until a skewer inserted into the center comes out clean. Let the loaf cool slightly.

4. To make the drizzle, mix together the maple syrup and cinnamon in a small bowl. Drizzle over the loaf, cut into slices, and serve warm or completely cooled. Store in an airtight container at room temperature for up to 5 days or freeze for 2 months.

*TOP TIP
Sandwich two slices of this together with a nut butter filling, pop it into a container, and you've got a takeaway breakfast on the run!

* TOP TIP
Double up the quantities
to make a double-layered
delight, using the frosting
as a filling as well as for
topping the cake.

GOLDEN SPICED CARROT CAKE

Turmeric is having a moment; the orangey spice has been re-colored as "golden" to sound much more majestic. The "golden" fairy dust is everywhere. In a latte? Yes please! Added to all savory dishes? Sure! When it comes to baking, turmeric and carrots are a color match made in heaven. Topped with a creamy coconutty frosting, we're talking more than heavenly. Thanks to the turmeric this cake is also anti-inflammatory and even one of your five-a-day! Eating it is a bit like finding a pot of yellowy-orange at the end of a rainbow . . . ✳ MAKES 1 CAKE (ABOUT 10 SLICES)

2 cups ground almonds
⅓ cup buckwheat flour
1 tablespoon ground cinnamon
1 teaspoon pumpkin pie spice
1 teaspoon ground turmeric
1½ cups finely grated carrots
⅓ cup pure maple syrup
2 tablespoons coconut oil, melted

FOR THE GOLDEN FROSTING
½ cup chilled full-fat coconut milk (see page 12)
¼ cup pure maple syrup
¼ cup coconut oil, melted
½ teaspoon ground turmeric

1. Preheat the oven to 350°F. Line an 8-inch round cake pan with parchment paper.

2. Mix together the ground almonds, buckwheat flour, and pumpkin pie spice in a mixing bowl. Add the carrots, maple syrup, and melted coconut oil and stir until sticky. Spoon the mixture evenly into the lined pan and bake for 25 minutes, or until turning golden on top and a skewer inserted into the center comes out clean. Let cool while you make the frosting.

3. Mix together all the frosting ingredients, then spoon onto the cooled cake. Store in the fridge for up to 3 days or freeze for 2 months.

CHOCOLATE ZUCCHINI CAKE

Without eggs, baked goods can end up a little dry unless something else contributes moisture, so I love experimenting with fruits, veggies, and legumes in their place. I had some zucchini lying around once and had to find a way to use them before they went bad, and as it turns out, zucchini works well in a good old chocolate cake. You obviously lose the green color when the vegetable's grated and blended into the batter, so I've added a coconut-matcha frosting as a little nod to all things green ✳ MAKES 1 CAKE (ABOUT 10 SLICES)

1 zucchini, finely grated
1½ cups ground almonds
1 cup pitted Medjool dates
⅓ cup cacao powder
⅓ cup desiccated coconut
1½ cups coconut milk
pinch of Himalayan pink salt (optional)

FOR THE MATCHA-COCONUT FROSTING
½ cup chilled full-fat coconut milk (see page 12)
2 tablespoons pure maple syrup
1 teaspoon matcha green tea powder

1. Preheat the oven to 350°F. Line an 8-inch round cake pan with parchment paper.

2. Process all the cake ingredients except the zucchini in a food processor until smooth. Spoon into a mixing bowl, add the grated zucchini, and mix well.

3. Pour into the lined pan and bake for 25 minutes, or until a skewer inserted into the center comes out clean. Let cool while you make the frosting.

4. To make the frosting, mix together all the ingredients in a mixing bowl. Place in the fridge for an hour to firm up, then spoon onto the cake. Store in the fridge for up to 3 days or freeze for 2 months.

NOTELLA-FILLED BANANA BREAD

I firmly believe that you are what you eat, in which case I've clearly been eating far too much of this, as I'm definitely a little nuts and bananas!

A moist, gooey banana bread is so delicious on its own, but in a (rare) moment of genius I realized what would make it even better—a hazelnut-chocolate middle running through it and flecked with cacao nibs. This quickly became a staple item on my market stall and sold out week after week, so I guess I'm not the only one who's a little crazy for this pimped-up, choco-fied banana bread delight.

✱ MAKES 1 LOAF (ABOUT 8 GENEROUS SLICES)

4 very ripe large bananas, peeled
1 cup buckwheat flour
1 cup ground almonds
7 tablespoons pure maple syrup
2 tablespoons chia seeds
2 tablespoons ground cinnamon
1 cup pecans
3 tablespoons cacao nibs
   (or small chunks of Raw Dark Chocolate;
   see page 31)
1 batch Hazelnut-Chocolate Spread (page 20)

1. Preheat the oven to 350°F. Line a 6 by 4-inch loaf pan with parchment paper.

2. Mash the bananas in a mixing bowl. Add the buckwheat flour, ground almonds, maple syrup, chia seeds, and cinnamon and stir together well.

3. Process the pecans in a food processor for about 30 seconds, or until they have the texture of coarse flour, then add to the bowl with the banana mixture. Add the cacao nibs (or chocolate chunks) and give it all another good stir.

4. Spoon half the banana mixture into the lined loaf pan and smooth the top with the spoon. Cover with a layer of the hazelnut-chocolate spread, again smoothing it out to make it all nice and even. Spoon the remaining banana mixture on top and smooth it out once more.

5. Bake for an hour, or until a skewer inserted into the center comes out clean. If there is chocolate on the skewer, don't worry, as the filling is meant to be slightly gooey; as long as the banana loaf mixture is cooked, that's fine. Let the loaf cool, then slice. Store in an airtight container in the fridge for up to 5 days or freeze for 2 months.

BANOFFEE SURPRISE CUPCAKES

I'm a sucker for things with fillings—I think it's something to do with the texture. Back in the day when I was a self-confessed sugar fiend, I would wolf down all manner of filled muffins, cakes, and doughnuts. Recently I was reminded of my love for things with gooey centers and, feeling inspired, I got in the kitchen (well, I stayed in the kitchen, as I'm always in the kitchen) and came up with these mouth-watering banoffee beauties. Besides their secret salted caramel insides, there is frosting to be enjoyed here, too, combining the creaminess of banana with the richness of chocolate.

✱ MAKES 9 CUPCAKES

FOR THE CUPCAKE BATTER
4 ripe bananas
1 cup buckwheat flour
1½ cups ground almonds
2 flaxseed "eggs" (see page 13)
1 cup almond milk (see page 18)
⅓ cup pure maple syrup
⅓ cup coconut oil, melted

FOR THE SALTED CARAMEL FILLING
⅔ cup pitted Medjool dates
½ cup almond milk (see page 18)
pinch of Himalayan pink salt

FOR THE BANANA-CHOCOLATE FROSTING
1½ cups chilled full-fat coconut milk (see page 12)
3 tablespoons pure maple syrup
1½ tablespoons cacao powder
2 ripe bananas, peeled

1. Preheat the oven to 350°F. Line nine wells of a muffin tin with paper liners.

2. To make the batter, blend the bananas in a blender until totally smooth. Pour into a mixing bowl and stir in the buckwheat flour, ground almonds, and flaxseed "eggs." Add the almond milk, maple syrup, and melted coconut oil and stir until everything is mixed together.

3. To make the filling, process all the ingredients in a food processor or high-speed blender for 1 to 2 minutes, until a sticky, gooey caramel forms. It may be a little runny, but will harden a little during baking.

4. Spoon 2 tablespoons of the batter into each prepared well of the muffin tin, then add 1 tablespoon of the filling to each and top with 2 tablespoons more batter.

5. Bake the cupcakes for about 25 minutes, or until a skewer inserted into the center comes out clean. Let cool for an hour or so, then it's time to get frosting!

6. To make the frosting, process the coconut milk, maple syrup, cacao powder, and 1½ bananas in the food processor until smooth. Spoon or pipe the frosting on top of the cupcakes. Slice the reserved ½ banana and use it to garnish the frosted cupcakes. Store in the fridge for up to 5 days or freeze for 2 months.

LEMON FOR SHIZZLE MY DRIZZLE CAKE

Lemon drizzle cake is one of those traditionally British baked goods that, in my opinion, no afternoon tea is quite complete without. It's definitely one of my top five and therefore ended up as one of the four layers of our wedding cake (each layer was a different flavor, as we couldn't possibly choose just one). Mr. H and I sat in our wedding venue the morning after, eating the different kinds of cake with our fingers for breakfast and discussing the real-life fairy tale that had been our wedding day, and I think the lemon drizzle may have been my favorite.

It has the loveliest mix of flavors: light sponge with a hint of zesty lemon, drizzled with a seductively sweet lemony icing. The addition of poppy seeds gives it a fabulous texture, too. ✶ MAKES 1 LOAF (ABOUT 8 SLICES)

1 cup gluten-free rolled oats
1½ cups ground almonds
½ cup coconut sugar
2 tablespoons chia seeds
1 cup almond milk (see page 18)
⅓ cup coconut oil, melted
finely grated zest and juice of 1 lemon
1 teaspoon pure vanilla extract
¼ cup poppy seeds

FOR THE DRIZZLE
2 tablespoons fresh lemon juice
1 tablespoon pure maple syrup
1 tablespoon coconut milk

1. Preheat the oven to 350°F. Line a 6 by 4-inch loaf pan with parchment paper.

2. Process the oats in a food processor or high-speed blender for about 30 seconds, or until they form a flour. Mix with the ground almonds, coconut sugar, and chia seeds in a mixing bowl.

3. Stir in the almond milk, melted coconut oil, lemon zest and juice, and vanilla until well combined, then stir in the poppy seeds.

4. Spoon the mixture evenly into the lined loaf pan and bake for 30 to 35 minutes, until golden on top and a skewer inserted into the center comes out clean. Let the cake cool before you make the drizzle.

5. When the cake is cool, to make the drizzle, stir all the drizzle ingredients together in a mixing bowl until smooth, then drizzle over the top of the cake and dig in! Store leftovers in the fridge for up to 3 days or freeze for 2 months.

PINEAPPLE UPSIDE-DOWN LOAF

When I was younger, my brother and I would dig holes in the garden to try and reach Australia. My dad (who loved to take advantage of our gullibility) told us that if we did go down under, everything would be upside down and we would have to wear sticky shoes or else we would fall off the world. We did visit Australia when I was eleven, whereupon we discovered that neither of those things was true. I went again with Mr. H and Baby H a couple of years ago to visit my brother and his wife who were living there, and while there we had the most delicious pineapple cake. It made me laugh because in the UK we would have called it an upside-down cake, but in Sydney it was simply "cake." Was this because they are upside down already, and therefore, the cake wasn't?

What I do know is that this cake is pure pineapple heaven. By cooking it with the fruit at the bottom, then turning it over once baked, the sweet, juicy pineapple flavors infuse the rest of the loaf, making it one hell of a dessert.

✳ MAKES 1 LOAF (ABOUT 8 SLICES)

¾ cup almond milk (see page 18)
1 tablespoon apple cider vinegar
1½ cups ground almonds
1 flaxseed "egg" (see page 13)
½ cup cashew butter (see tip, page 22)
½ cup coconut oil, melted
½ cup plus 2 tablespoons pure maple syrup
1 teaspoon pure vanilla extract
⅓ pineapple, peeled, cored, and
   cut into 2 or 3 thin rings

1. Preheat the oven to 350°F. Line a 6 by 4-inch loaf pan with parchment paper.

2. Mix together the almond milk and apple cider vinegar in a mixing bowl and set aside. In another mixing bowl, mix the ground almonds with the flaxseed "egg," then stir in the cashew butter, melted coconut oil, ½ cup of the maple syrup, and the vanilla until well combined.

3. Pour the remaining 2 tablespoons maple syrup over the bottom of the prepared loaf pan, place the pineapple rings over the syrup, then pour in the cake batter. Bake for 50 minutes, or until a skewer inserted into the center of the cake comes out clean.

4. Let the cake cool in the pan, then place a plate over the loaf pan and, holding them both together, flip the pan so that the cake sits on the plate, with the pineapple at the top. Store in the fridge for up to 3 days or freeze for 2 months.

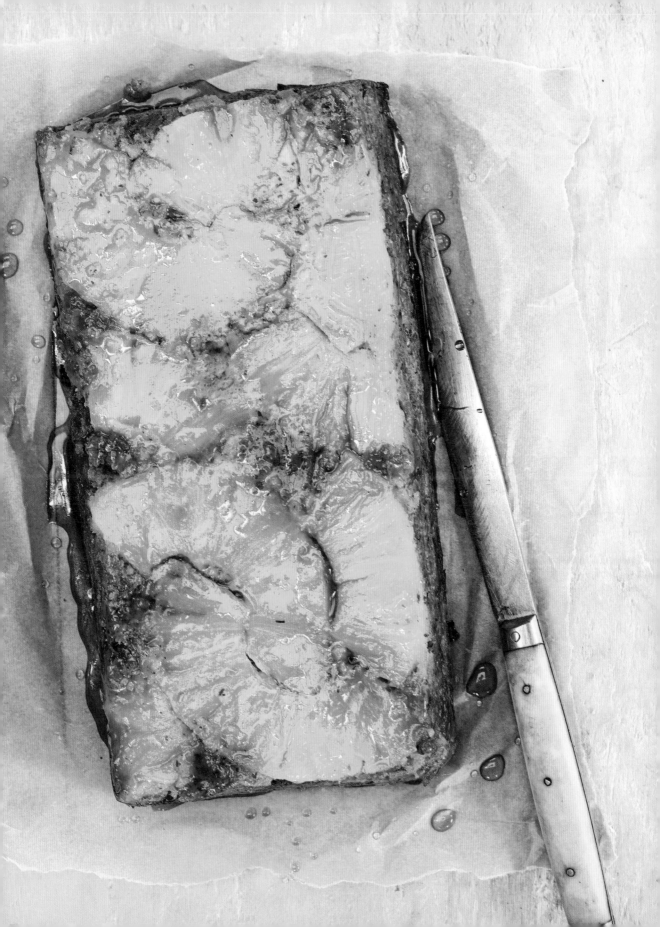

RED VELVET CAKE

It makes me so sad if I ever have to throw food away at the end of the week that I make every effort to plan our meals in advance. However, I still end up with the odd item that needs using up in some way, and recently it was beet. In a moment of cake clarity it came to me—why not try my hand at healthy red velvet? Traditional red velvet cakes are actually colored with beet and I love its earthy, rich texture, so I figured that adding it to a cake could only be a good idea. It also helps keep the cake lovely and moist, and gives it a wonderfully light, spongy texture.

Red velvet needs to be smothered with cream cheese frosting (I think it's the law in some countries), so I've whipped up a vegan version that I promise will not disappoint.

✳ MAKES 1 CAKE (ABOUT 10 SLICES)

2 tablespoons ground flaxseeds
½ cup almond milk (see page 18)
1 cup cacao powder
½ cup ground almonds
½ cup almond butter
½ cup pure maple syrup
8 Medjool dates, pitted
6 tablespoons coconut oil
2 raw beets, peeled and chopped into chunks
1 batch Cream "Cheese" Frosting (page 24)
pinch of beet powder, for garnish (optional)

1. Preheat the oven to 350°F. Line an 8-inch round cake pan with parchment paper.

2. Place the flaxseeds in a small cup, add the almond milk, and let soak for 10 minutes.

3. Pour the flaxseed–almond milk mixture into a food processor and add the cacao powder, ground almonds, almond butter, maple syrup, dates, coconut oil, and chopped beets. Process for about 5 minutes, or until smooth, stopping every couple of minutes to give the mixture a good stir.

4. Spoon the mixture evenly into the lined cake pan and bake for 30 minutes, or until a skewer inserted into the center comes out clean. Transfer the cake to a wire rack to cool for at least 30 minutes while you make and chill the frosting.

5. Prepare the cream "cheese" frosting following the recipe on page 24. The result should be super smooth and creamy, not to mention delicious! Place it in the fridge for 20 minutes to firm up (otherwise, it will be too loose to pipe), then spoon it into a piping bag and frost away! Garnish the cake with the beet powder, if desired. Store in the fridge for up to 5 days or freeze for 2 months.

Special-occasion cakes to knock their socks off

My blog and recipes are all about making healthier, delicious sweet treats easy and accessible for everyone. But what about when it comes to birthdays and other celebrations? Do you buy a store-bought cake for a reasonable price even though it might have a list of questionable ingredients as long as your arm? Or do you order one that meets your dietary requirements from a specialist baker, which may cost you considerably more than if you had made it yourself? You don't have to do either—I'm about to show you how to make fabulous, showstopping cakes on a budget in the comfort of your own home.

Since starting Mrs. Hollingsworth's, I've made hundreds of celebration cakes for many wonderful customers, so here I'm sharing with you my most popular special-occasion cake, as well as the beautiful tiered design I created for Baby H's first birthday, and last but not least, my take on everyone's favorite, the caterpillar cake. I've also included step-by-step instructions to guide you through decorating any cake to create your very own Pinterest-worthy masterpieces. So get frosting, drizzling, dripping, piping, and . . . licking the bowl, because that's mandatory. Use this guide to decorate your cakes and create showstopping wonders of your own!

STEP 1
RAW CHOCOLATE DRIPS AND DROPS

I don't think anything can beat the allure of chocolate dripping down a delicious cake. It looks so luxurious and indulgent, but it's incredibly easy to do.

1 batch White, Milk, or Dark Raw Chocolate (page 31), melted
cacao nibs (optional)
freeze-dried strawberry or raspberry pieces (optional)
Peanut Butter Crunch Balls (page 37; optional)
Melt-in-the-Middle Chocolate Truffles (page 122; optional)

Using a teaspoon, gently spoon the molten chocolate around the edge of the cake so that it drips down the side. Sprinkle on cacao nibs or freeze-dried berries, or place peanut butter crunch balls or chocolate truffles around the edge of the cake, using the melted chocolate as glue to hold them in place.

*TOP TIP
This works best when your cake has been chilled in the fridge or freezer, as the chocolate will harden onto the cake quicker.

STEP 2
DELICIOUS DECORATIONS

When it comes to decorating a raw masterpiece, the more toppings, the better! I like to chop up things like brownies and homemade chocolate bars to use on top of my cakes. They make a great addition, and you can prepare them in advance and store them in the freezer until you need them. My favorite items are:

Hazelnut Raw-No-Shares
   (page 125)
Peanut Butter Cups (page 120)
"Snick" Me Another Peanut
   Caramel Bars (page 124),
   chopped into chunks
The World's Best Brownies,
   (page 53) cut into chunks
Peanut Butter Crunch Balls
   (page 37), shaped into
   different-sized balls, some
   drizzled with chocolate and
   some plain
Raw White Chocolate (page 31),
   in heart or star shapes,
   to add a little color variation
   among all the brown

Alternatively, if you don't have time to make these, you can use store-bought balls and bars and chop them up into chunks to add variety to your cakes.

STEP 3
PUTTING IT ALL TOGETHER

This is where you can get super creative. Take all your decorations and arrange them on your cake. You can build them up into a mountain, put them around the edge (great if you want to add a message in the center), or position them in a crescent shape around the outside. I find balls work best for creating a mountain structure, and my favorites to use are:

Hazelnut Raw No-Shares (page 125)
Peanut Butter Crunch Balls (page 37)

Place one ball in the middle and arrange a circle of balls around it (I usually use 5 or 6 for this) to form the base layer, sticking them down with some melted raw chocolate. Place another 3 or 4 balls on top and then one final ball on top of the second layer. Stick on other decorations, such as Chocolate Truffles (page 122) or chunks of Peanut Caramel Bars (page 124), to fill in any gaps and make your mountain look totally drool-worthy.

Once you're happy with the arrangement, stick each one down with some melted raw chocolate to ensure everything stays in place.

STEP 4
THE FINISHING TOUCHES

Raw cakes can tend to look a bit monotone, especially chocolate ones, so it's nice to add some color if possible. I like to add color with:

frosting (see page 155)–this can
   be piped to make little flowers
   or stars in different colors
edible petals and leaves (rose,
   marigold, mint, and cornflower
   are my favorites)
dried fruit (goji berries,
   cranberries, and apricots are
   all good)
freeze-dried berries (most
   supermarkets sell strawberry
   and raspberry pieces in the
   cake-decorating aisle)
fresh berries (these can only
   be added just before serving,
   as they don't stay fresh for
   very long)
flowers (not to eat but to look
   pretty, especially for wedding
   cakes)
gold dust or gold foil (natural
   versions that contain only
   minerals and gold are available
   online, great for adding a
   glamorous final flourish)

STEP 5
EAT!

Because cake decorating is hungry work.

MY STAPLE CELEBRATION CAKE

I started out just making cakes for friends and family to get some feedback on what worked and what didn't. I created this for Mr. H's thirty-first birthday and spent ages photographing it, trying to get the best shot to share on my Instagram and blog. It was worth the effort, as not long after I posted the picture people began to inquire whether they could order it for themselves. And thus, the peanut butter cup brownie chocolate fudge "cheesecake" was born—a bit of a mouthful, but so is this cake.

The original peanut butter version is still up there in the popularity stakes, but probably equally as popular is the chocolate "cheesecake" style. I know lots of people don't eat or like peanuts, so I've shared both recipes so that you can choose your favorite. Or why not go all out and do one layer of each? ✳ MAKES 1 CAKE (ABOUT 12 SLICES)

FOR THE BROWNIE LAYER

3 tablespoons coconut oil, plus extra for greasing
1⅓ cups drained and rinsed canned black beans
⅔ cup pitted Medjool dates
½ cup gluten-free rolled oats
½ cup cacao powder
½ cup classic almond milk (see page 18)
2 tablespoons ground flaxseeds

OPTION 1 FOR THE PEANUT BUTTER "CHEESECAKE" LAYER

1 cup peanut butter (see page 21)
1 cup pitted Medjool dates
¼ cup coconut oil
1 cup classic almond milk (see page 18)
pinch of Himalayan pink salt

OPTION 2 FOR THE CHOCOLATE "CHEESECAKE" LAYER

1½ cups raw cashews, soaked in water for at least 4 hours, then drained
1½ cups coconut cream
1 cup pitted Medjool dates
1 ripe avocado, halved, pitted, and peeled
½ cup cacao powder
½ cup coconut oil, melted

FOR THE CHOCOLATE FUDGE TOPPING

½ cup cacao powder
½ cup pure maple syrup
½ cup peanut butter (see page 21)
½ cup coconut oil, melted

1. To make the brownie layer, preheat the oven to 350°F. Grease an 8-inch springform pan with coconut oil.

2. Process all the brownie ingredients in a food processor for a couple of minutes, or until smooth. Spoon the mixture into the prepared cake pan and bake for 35 to 40 minutes, until a skewer inserted into the center comes out clean. Let cool, then pop it in the freezer while you make the next layer.

3. To make the peanut butter or chocolate "cheesecake" layer, process all the ingredients in a food processor for about 3 minutes, or until smooth. Remove the brownie layer from the freezer and spoon the "cheesecake" mixture evenly over the top, smoothing it out with the spoon, then return it to the freezer for at least an hour to set. (If desired, repeat with the ingredients for the other layer, peanut butter or chocolate.)

4. To make the chocolate fudge topping, mix together all the ingredients in a mixing bowl until you have a thick, chocolaty mixture. Pour the mixture evenly over the "cheesecake" layer and return it to the freezer for an hour or so more to set. Remove the springform ring and decorate as desired just before serving. Store in a freezerproof container in the freezer for up to 2 months; remove 2 hours before serving.

THE QUINTESSENTIAL VICTORIA SPONGE

You can't really get a more English cake than a Victoria sponge. Popularized by and named after Queen Victoria, it has remained in favor ever since the monarch's long reign. For me, it conjures up lovely memories of stuffing my face at afternoon teas and picnicking in questionable weather.

This cake is packed full of amazing texture and flavor: fluffy vanilla cake with scrumptious berry jelly and an indulgent creamy filling makes for the most perfect of cakes. ✳ MAKES 1 CAKE (ABOUT 10 SLICES)

1 cup aquafaba (the liquid drained from two 14-ounce cans chickpeas)
1 cup pure maple syrup
¼ cup coconut oil, melted
2 teaspoons pure vanilla extract
1½ cups gluten-free rolled oats
3 cups ground almonds

FOR THE FILLING
1 cup chilled full-fat coconut milk (see page 12)
¼ cup pure maple syrup
Berry Chia Jelly (page 26), made with raspberries

coconut flour, desiccated coconut, and/or berries, for garnish

✳ TOP TIP
I tend to make a batch of the jelly in advance, as you can freeze it and then just defrost it before you want to bake.

1. Preheat the oven to 350°F. Line two 8-inch round cake pans with parchment paper.

2. Beat the aquafaba in a mixing bowl with a handheld mixer (or in the bowl of a stand mixer fitted with the whisk attachment) until it becomes light, white, and fluffy. Add the maple syrup, melted coconut oil, and vanilla and stir until mixed together.

3. Process the oats in a food processor or high-speed blender for about 1 minute, or until they form a fine flour. Gently fold the oats and the ground almonds into the aquafaba.

4. Divide the mixture between the lined cake pans and bake for 30 to 35 minutes, until starting to look golden brown on top and a skewer inserted into the center of each cake comes out clean. Let cool completely.

5. To make the filling, mix together the coconut milk and maple syrup in a mixing bowl.

6. Remove the cakes from the pans. Set one layer on a cake plate and spread the jelly over the top, then spread on the maple coconut cream. Top with the second cake layer. Decorate with coconut flour, desiccated coconut and/or berries, or leave it naked and just dig in! Store in the fridge for up to 3 days or freeze for 2 months.

CATERPILLAR CAKE

My brother is a firm believer that birthdays are not birthdays if they don't involve a caterpillar cake. It's a bit of a random idea if you think about it, but whoever thought to jazz up what is essentially a chocolate Swiss roll to make it look like a many-footed insect must be laughing all the way to the bank. It's become something of an institution, with every supermarket doing their take on it, so I thought it was only right to get in on the action.

This cake looks incredibly fancy, but I'll let you in on a little secret: it's actually not. All you need is a batch of brownies, some filling, a bit of raw chocolate, and some decorations. Want to totally impress your partygoers? Give it a go! * MAKES 1 CAKE (ABOUT 12 SLICES)

FOR THE COLORED FROSTING
1 cup raw cashews, soaked in
    water for 4 hours, then drained
1 cup coconut milk
¼ cup coconut oil
¼ cup pure maple syrup

NATURAL COLORINGS (OPTIONAL)
ground turmeric (yellow)
beet or pink pitaya powder (pink)
butterfly pea powder (blue)
wheatgrass powder (green)

1 batch Raw White Chocolate
    (page 31), for the feet and face

FOR THE CAKE
batter for 1 batch The World's Best Brownies
    (page 53)
½ batch Four-ingredient
    Chocolate Frosting (page 24)
1 batch Raw Dark Chocolate (page 31), melted

1. To make the frosting, process all the ingredients in a food processor for about 5 minutes until smooth. Divide among as many bowls as colors you're using, and stir ½ teaspoon of coloring into each. Add more to reach the tint you like. Chill for 4 hours to set.

2. To make the feet and face, pour the raw white chocolate into molds (use small circles cut in half for the feet and a larger circle for the face). Freeze to set.

3. To make the cake, preheat the oven to 300°F. Line a shallow 8-inch square baking pan with parchment paper, or use a silicone mold. Make the brownie batter following the recipe on page 53, spoon it into the prepared pan, and bake for 20 minutes. Let cool.

4. Carefully unmold the brownie onto a large sheet of parchment paper. Cover with the chocolate frosting, leaving a 1-inch-wide strip uncovered along the side farthest from you. Starting from the opposite side, use the parchment paper to roll the brownie into a cylinder, pressing down the non-frosted edge to seal. Neaten each end. Place the cake in the freezer to chill.

5. Pour the melted dark chocolate into a shallow dish. Dunk the chilled cake into the chocolate, turning to coat. Use any leftover to stick on the face and feet.

6. Put one frosting color in a piping bag fitted with a round tip and pipe dots on top of the cake. Repeat with all the colors. Use a little pink frosting to make the mouth.

*TOP TIP
To serve more people, make another batch of brownies to use as a flat "grass" base. Bake as above, then let cool and cover with green frosting (wheatgrass powder gives frosting a pale green tint). For an extra "grassy" effect, stir together some desiccated coconut and a little wheatgrass powder and sprinkle it on top.

BABY H'S RAW UNICORN CAKE

This cake is very sentimental to me, as I made it to celebrate Baby H's first birthday. I wanted to create something that was rich and indulgent, but featuring pastel colors and light vanilla flavors, as well as chocolate, of course. I created a three-tiered cake, with each layer having a chocolate brownie base and a swirly vanilla "cheesecake" topping, dripping with chocolate and covered in all my favorite decorations. It got demolished before we could even finish singing "Happy Birthday"!

This recipe makes one 8-inch cake, but to make an additional two tiers (4 and 6 inches in diameter, respectively), simply double the quantities. ✻ MAKES 1 CAKE (ABOUT 12 SLICES)

batter for 1 batch The World's Best Brownies (page 53)

FOR THE VANILLA "CHEESECAKE" LAYER
1 cup raw cashews, soaked in
    water for at least 4 hours, then drained
1 cup coconut milk
¼ cup pure maple syrup
¼ cup coconut oil
1 teaspoon pure vanilla extract

NATURAL COLORINGS (OPTIONAL)
beet or pink pitaya powder (pink)
butterfly pea powder (blue)
combination of beet or pink pitaya powder
    and butterfly pea powder (purple)

1. Preheat the oven to 300°F. Line an 8-inch springform pan with parchment paper.

2. Spoon the brownie batter into the lined cake pan and bake for 20 minutes. Allow to cool slightly, then place the cake in the freezer to cool completely while you make the "cheesecake" layer.

3. To make the vanilla "cheesecake" layer, process all the ingredients in a food processor for about 5 minutes, or until the mixture is creamy and smooth.

4. I use four colors when making this cake—white, pink, blue, and purple—so I divide the "cheesecake" mixture between four bowls, but if you are using a different number of colors, just split it into bowls accordingly. Stir ½ teaspoon coloring into each bowl of "cheesecake" mixture. Add more coloring if you want to darken the tint.

5. Remove the brownie from the freezer. Using a different tablespoon for each color and alternating colors, spoon heaping tablespoons of the "cheesecake" mixture onto the brownie until you have used all the colored mixtures. Take a skewer and swirl it through the "cheesecake" mixture to create a marbled effect (but don't swirl so much that the colors become indistinct). Place the cake in the fridge overnight to set, then remove from the pan and decorate however you wish!

✻ TOP TIP
If you've only got one color on hand (just beet powder, for example), you can create different shades by adding varying amounts of the powder to separate bowls of the "cheesecake" mixture, and swirl those together.

INDEX

THANK YOUS

At the risk of sounding like an Oscar winner (although I suppose that is how I feel right now), there are a number of people without whom this book simply wouldn't have been possible. A special mention to my husband Richard; thank you for giving up your time (and waistline) to help me make this happen, you are my rock. You've had my back every step of the way and I feel so lucky to have you by my side. And to my little Zari, thank you for light-ing up my life and always being there to help me lick the spoon. I hope this book will make you as proud of me as I am of you every day.

To my family; Brian, Fran, Jonathan, Nicole, Stephie, Lara, David, Sam, Suzanne, Graham, Juliet, Matt, Ezra and Shiloh – thank you for your babysitting, market stall visits and dessert eating, being my unofficial PR team and for your endless love and support.
Thank you also to my incredible friends old and new; I feel so blessed to know so many amazing people who always know how to make me smile.

To my wonderful cake customers, workshop attendees, blog readers and Instagram followers – I am so grateful to you all for allowing me to turn my passions into what I can only call the best job in the world. An extra thanks to my amazing kitchen angel Emma Tanner, you have helped me out more than you know!

Finally, thank you to everyone who worked on making this book as mouthwatering as it is; to the fabulous Jane and Jen at Graham Maw Christie, to the incredible team at Kyle Books, Jen Rich for her insane photography skills and Annie Rigg for styling the hell out of my recipes. Thank you also Helen Bratby for the design and Anne Sheasby for proofreading.

An Hachette UK Company
www.hachette.co.uk

This edition published 2019 by
Kyle Books, an imprint of Kyle Cathie Ltd
Carmelite House
50 Victoria Embankment
London EC4Y 0DZ
www.kylebooks.co.uk

ISBN: 978 0 85783 631 1

First published in Great Britain in 2019

Distributed in the US by Hachette Book Group, 1290 Avenue of the Americas, 4th and 5th Floors, New York, NY 10104

Distributed in Canada by Canadian Manda Group, 664 Annette St., Toronto, Ontario, Canada M6S 2C8

Editor **Hannah Coughlin**
Designer **Helen Bratby**
Photographer **Jen Rich**
Food Stylist **Annie Rigg**
Prop Stylist **Agathe Gits**
Production **Nic Jones** and **Gemma John**

Printed and bound in China

10 9 8 7 6 5 4 3 2 1